Home Café

100 Recipes for Irresistible Coffees and Delectable Desserts

Aileen A. Anastacio

Marshall Cavendish
Cuisine

Editor: Lydia Leong
Designer: Rachel Chen Choon Jet
Photographer: Robby Sibal

Published by Marshall Cavendish Cuisine
An imprint of Marshall Cavendish International
1 New Industrial Road, Singapore 536196

Other Marshall Cavendish Offices:

Marshall Cavendish Ltd. PO Box 65829, London, EC1P 1NY, UK • Marshall Cavendish Corporation,
99 White Plains Road, Tarrytown NY 10591-9001, USA • Marshall Cavendish International (Thailand)
Co Ltd. 253 Asoke, 12th Flr, Sukhumvit 21 Road, Klongtoey Nua, Wattana, Bangkok 10110, Thailand
• Marshall Cavendish (Malaysia) Sdn Bhd, Times Subang, Lot 46, Subang Hi-Tech Industrial Park,
Batu Tiga, 40000 Shah Alam, Selangor Darul Ehsan, Malaysia

Marshall Cavendish is a trademark of Times Publishing Limited

National Library Board Singapore Cataloguing in Publication Data

Anastacio, Aileen A.
Home cafe : 100 recipes for irresistible coffees and delectable desserts / Aileen A. Anastacio. – Singapore :
Marshall Cavendish Cuisine, c2010.
p. cm.
ISBN-13 : 978-981-4276-09-2

1. Coffee. 2. Confectionery. I. Title.

TX817.C6
641.877 -- dc22   OCN462392530

Printed in Singapore by Times Printers Pte Ltd

Dedication

This book is for you Mom.
Your love and support have kept me going.
I hope that I have made you proud.

And to my sweetie, my dear Sabrina,
you never fail to make me smile!
I am looking forward to baking with you,
and as we enjoy our desserts together,
it's going to be with coffee for me
and milk, in the meantime, for you!

Contents

Acknowledgements

This book would not have been realised without the help of several very talented people. Their passion and love for their craft can be seen in this book.

Robby Sibal, whom I have enjoyed working with for almost nine years now, your photographs just keep on getting better and better. Not only are you my first choice when it comes to a photographer, but you make work so much fun.

Angelo Comsti, for your labour of love, for your creativity in food styling and for being an amazing writer too. You have made all the drinks and desserts look as attractive as they are delectable.

Jacquiline Franquelli, a brilliant writer in your own right, with several books under your belt. A big hug to you for helping me rewrite and edit my recipes. When I am at a loss for words, you always come to the rescue.

Equilibrium Intertrade Corporation, distributor of Mauro Coffee and Torani flavoured syrups, for supporting me in this endeavour. Our *The Flavored Cup* book is just the beginning of many more good cups of coffee together. The quality of your products has resulted in the creation of the many wonderful drinks in this book.

Family and friends—my sister Vivian and brother Lloyd, in-laws Butch and Rhea, friends Marivic, Anna, Cathy and Ton—who willingly volunteered to make constructive comments to improve and shortlist the recipes in this book.

And most importantly, my deepest gratitude to God, my creator, for giving me the talent and the gift to create, and for moulding me to be who I am today.

Introduction

It was five years ago, when I scribbled my to-do list for the coming years in my little notebook. The list included recipes I wanted to create, foods I wanted to try and desserts I wanted to bake. But life got so busy that I had no time to work on any of those tasks.

In the past year alone, I was involved in two projects. One was a 20-recipe book called *The Flavored Cup*, a product of 10 years of teaching basic espresso-making and dessert coffee classes. It was a career-first for me, thanks to the Equilibrium Intertrade Corporation who sponsored the project.

The other project involved another passion of mine, desserts. A television producer was searching for two female chefs who owned bakeshops and who had a teaching background. And since I fit the bill, I was asked to co-host a baking show called *True Confections*. I was initially apprehensive because I was unsure how much of my time would be taken up, but when I found out that taping would only be once a month, I happily agreed. We started taping mid-August 2008 and the show was launched two months after. It was a success! The ratings were high and we had a loyal following. Many viewers also often left questions and comments on the show's blog site (trueconfection.multiply.com) where the recipes were posted. This overwhelming interest and positive response inspired me to take on yet another project—a cookbook of coffee and dessert recipes— which you now hold in your hands.

This book includes recipes that were favourites among viewers of *True Confections*, as well as some of my own indulgences. And to complete the sugar-high experience, I match them with a variety of espresso drinks, from the hot and the iced, to those filled with creams and ice cream (which I call dessert coffees) and those with a touch of alcohol (which I call cocktail coffees).

This collection of recipes materialised last Mother's Day when my family and I spent lazy days and cold nights up at Baguio City, in the Philippines. While having an extended lunch, I asked each family member what sweet treat they constantly crave for and the types of coffee they typically pair their choices with. Their responses made up my initial list, which was then made more complete when I got feedback from friends and clients as well. The result is this— 50 tried-and-tested recipes for baked goodies and 50 delicious coffee concoctions.

With these recipes, I hope to introduce you to a variety of coffee drinks that can be easily made and enjoyed at home. The same goes for the desserts. This book includes a wide range of pastries, from delectable cookies to sinful cakes that are not only easy to do, but also very easy to indulge in. I believe that life is too short to have a bad coffee or a lousy dessert, so it's time you made your kitchen a home café where good coffee and desserts can be found.

While working on this book, I sorted through old files and memory banks for recipes. And as I was going through my piles of books, there I saw it—my little notebook containing my to-do list. In a funny twist of fate, it included doing a cookbook of coffee and desserts, which I can now tick off the list.

And I hope you too can cross off baking and coffee-making in your own bucket list with the help of this book. So put on your aprons and start having fun in the kitchen!

The Basics

What Makes a Good Espresso

There are several factors that affect the quality of the espresso, but it all starts from having good beans.

Good Beans

- A good bean would have been grown in areas where there is an abundance of sunshine, moderate rainfall, an all-year round temperature of 70°F (20°C) and no frost.

- There are several species of coffee plants and the coffee beans they produce have their own different characteristics. Two main species of coffee that are cultivated today are Robusta coffee and Arabica coffee.

- Robusta grows in the lowlands. It is a robust plant that is resistant to diseases, giving a higher yield per plant. The beans are small and round, and the coffee that it produces has a higher caffeine content and harsher quality compared to Arabica.

- Arabica has a slower growing cycle than the Robusta. It is an elongated bean that grows on the highlands, hence it is also known as a "high-grown bean". When roasted, it produces a more flavourful and refined coffee compared to Robusta.

Right Roast

- The second factor to making a good espresso is having the right kind of roast. Nothing affects the flavour of the beans more than the roasting. An espresso roast is a roast that is very dark in colour, almost black, and is characterised by an oily surface on the beans.

Good Grind

- A third factor would be the grinds. A fine grind is perfect for a good extraction using the espresso machine. This will result in a good crema and a good shot of espresso.

Right Proportion of Grinds

- The fourth factor is measuring and using the correct proportion of grinds. A single shot of espresso requires 2 Tbsp (¼ to ⅓ oz / 7 to 9 g) of finely ground espresso coffee.

Clean Water, Right Temperature

- A fifth factor is to use clean, filtered water heated to the right temperature, 195°F (90°C).

Preheated Espresso Machine

- A final but no less important factor is to preheat the espresso machine before using it to extract the espresso (page 16).

Follow these guidelines and you will be on your way to making the perfect espresso in no time!

A perfect shot of espresso is pleasant and rich in flavour, not bitter. It will also have a thick layer of hazelnut-coloured foam known as crema on the top.

Espresso is traditionally served in a demitasse and is best served immediately after it has been extracted from the espresso machine.

Substitute for the Espresso Machine

Although nothing can really compare with the quality of espresso that a good espresso machine can produce, this is what you can do to make a really strong coffee, if you do not own an espresso machine.

With a plunger pot or a French press:

1. Measure out 2 Tbsp (¼ to ⅓ oz / 7 to 9 g) of ground espresso (medium grind) into the pot.

2. Add ¼ cup (2 fl oz / 60 ml) of freshly boiled water. Stir to mix. Place the plunger in loosely, just to cover and hold the heat in. Allow to steep for 3 to 4 minutes.

3. Hold the pot by the handle and slowly press down the plunger to hold the grounds down to the bottom of the pot.

4. Pour and measure out 1 shot (3 Tbsp / 1½ fl oz / 45 ml) of the strong coffee and use in place of the espresso shot in the recipes.

Heating and Frothing Milk
on a Stovetop or in a Saucepan

Milk can be steamed and frothed up using the
steam wand attached to espresso machines.
However, a saucepan and whisk will do just as well.

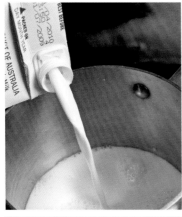

1. Half-fill a saucepan with cold
   milk. (Whole or full cream milk
   froth the best.)

2. Place the saucepan over medium
   heat to warm the milk. Use a
   wire whisk to stir the milk slowly.
   An electric hand-held mixer or
   blender can be used to speed up
   the process.

3. Start to whisk the milk as it
   warms up, increasing your speed
   as the milk rises in temperature.

4. Do not allow the milk to boil.
   Remove the saucepan from the
   heat from time to time to prevent
   it from boiling. If the milk boils,
   you will lose the froth and the
   texture of the milk will be grainy.

Making Espresso with an Espresso Machine

1. Preheat the espresso machine. Preheating the machine is like starting up the car before you use it. The pressure of the machine should be between 8 to 9 bars.

2. Test the machine by running water through the machine without coffee to make sure that it is running well.

3. Measure out about 2 Tbsp (¼ to ⅓ oz / 7 to 9 g) of finely ground espresso beans in a filter insert.

4. Tamp the coffee down slightly but firmly.

5. Clean the sides of the filter insert and brush off any excess grinds.

6. Clamp the filter securely into the espresso machine.

7. Move the handle from left to right, stopping at the centre to securely lock the handle.

8. Place warmed cups underneath the spout. Press the start button to extract the espresso.

9. The total extraction time should be between 20 and 25 seconds. Each shot of extracted espresso should be 3 Tbsp (1½ fl oz / 45 ml) with a good amount of crema.

Steaming and Frothing Milk with an Espresso Machine

1. Pour cold milk into a cold steam pitcher until about one-third full. (Whole or full cream milk froth the best.)

2. Bleed (turn the wand on and off to clear any residual milk) and clean the steam wand before inserting it into the milk.

3. Insert the tip of the steam wand (the nozzle) into the milk, placing it just below the milk surface.

4. Open the steam valve completely to start steaming the milk.

5. There will be a whirlpool effect, creating small bubbles and a smooth hissing sound will be produced.

6. Avoid positioning the nozzle too deep, as this will only result in heating the milk instead of creating froth.

7. Let the froth build, keeping the tip of the nozzle right below or beneath the surface.

8. Once the milk and froth fill up to three-quarters of the pitcher, drop the tip of the steam nozzle down into the centre to finish heating the milk.

9. Close the steam valve and let the pitcher of steamed milk set while you make your shots of espresso. This will give the froth time to settle.

10. Wipe the nozzle after steaming milk. Run a little steam to clear the nozzle of any milk residue.

   Tip: It is best to keep the temperature of the steamed milk at 140° to 150°F (60° to 65°C).

Making Cappuccino

1. Prepare the steamed milk and froth.

2. Extract a shot of espresso.

3. Pour the steamed milk gently into the middle of the espresso.

4. After pouring in the required amount of milk, gradually spoon in the froth to fill the cup.

Creating the Layered Effect

1. Prepare the steamed milk and froth.

2. Extract a shot of espresso.

3. Pour the chocolate syrup into a coffee cup.

4. Add the steamed milk.

5. Spoon in the froth.

6. Add the espresso, dribbling it slowly against the back of a spoon to create a layer of coffee.

7. Add additional froth as necessary to fill the cup.

Chocolate Etching

1. Make small drops of chocolate syrup on the froth. The layer of froth must be thick enough so the chocolate syrup does not sink into the espresso.

2. In one continuous motion, drag a toothpick or any pointed object down the middle of the drops to create a pattern.

3. Other patterns can be created by drawing parallel lines or concentric circles with the chocolate syrup, and dragging a toothpick or pointed object across the lines.

Latte Art: Heart

1. Prepare the steamed milk.

2. Extract a shot of espresso.

3. Pour the steamed milk slowly and gently into the middle of the espresso.

4. Add enough steamed milk to fill the cup up to three-quarters full.

5. Move the pitcher with the steamed milk back and forth and finish off with a stream of milk that will cut through from the centre to the edge of the cup to create the pointed edge of the heart.

Latte Art: Pinwheel

1. Prepare the steamed milk.

2. Extract a shot of espresso.

3. Pour the steamed milk slowly and gently into the middle of the espresso.

4. Add enough steamed milk to fill the cup.

5. Dip the tip of a toothpick or pointed object into the crema and drag it towards the centre of the cup in a curved line. Wipe off the tip of the toothpick or pointed object and repeat this action several times until you achieve the intended design.

Latte Art: Leaf Or Rosetta

1. Prepare the steamed milk.

2. Extract a shot of espresso.

3. Tilt the cup as you pour in the steamed milk so that the crema will surface on one side.

4. Move the pitcher from side to side to make a zigzag pattern as you level the cup.

5. Finish off with a stream of milk that will cut through the zigzag pattern to create the central vein of the leaf.

Tips to Measuring Ingredients

Plain (All-purpose) Flour

- Stir the flour in its storage container or bag to fluff it up, then use a big spoon to scoop the flour into the required measuring cup, so it overflows slightly. Do not compact the flour. Run the back of a knife or a spatula over the flour to level it off with the top edge of the measuring cup. One cup of flour should be about 4 oz (120 g).

Cake flour

- Sift the cake flour before measuring it as described above.

Granulated Sugar

- Stir the sugar in its storage container to break up any lumps, then use a big spoon to scoop the sugar into the required measuring cup, so it overflows slightly. Run the back of a knife or a spatula over the sugar to level it off with the top edge of the measuring cup. One cup of granulated sugar should be about 7 oz (200 g).

Brown Sugar

- Stir the sugar in its storage container to break up any lumps, then pack the sugar tightly into the required measuring cup. The sugar should hold the shape of the measuring cup when it is inverted.

Icing (Confectioner's) Sugar

- Sift the sugar first to remove any lumps. Measure it as you would granulated sugar. One cup of icing sugar should be about 4 oz (120 g).

Liquids

- Pour the liquid into a clear glass or plastic liquid measuring cup placed on a level surface. Bend down to read the measurement at eye level.

Metric and Imperial Measurement Equivalents

Quantities for this book are given in American spoon and cup measures. The Metric and Imperial measurement equivalents for these spoon and cup measures are listed here.

Dry Measures

Metric	Imperial
15 g	½ oz
30 g	1 oz
45 g	1½ oz
60 g	2 oz
75 g	2½ oz
90 g	3 oz
105 g	3½ oz
120 g	4 oz
180 g	6 oz
225 g	8 oz
285 g	10 oz
340 g	12 oz
400 g	14 oz
455 g	16 oz (1 lb)

Liquid and Volume Measures

Metric	Imperial	Spoon/Cup
5 ml	⅙ fl oz	1 tsp
15 ml	½ fl oz	1 Tbsp
30 ml	1 fl oz	2 Tbsp
45 ml	1½ fl oz	3 Tbsp (1 shot)
60 ml	2 fl oz	¼ cup
90 ml	3 fl oz	⅜ cup
120 ml	4 fl oz	½ cup
180 ml	6 fl oz	¾ cup
240 ml	8 fl oz	1 cup
300 ml	10 fl oz	1¼ cups
360 ml	12 fl oz	1½ cups
480 ml	16 fl oz	2 cups
600 ml	20 fl oz	2½ cups
720 ml	24 fl oz	3 cups
840 ml	28 fl oz	3½ cups
960 ml	32 fl oz	4 cups

Ingredients in 1 cup

Ingredient	Metric	Imperial
Almonds, sliced	90 g	3 oz
Almonds, whole	150 g	5 oz
Butter	225 g	8 oz
Chocolate chips	180 g	6 oz
Chocolate, chopped	180 g	6 oz
Chocolate cookie crumbs	120 g	4 oz
Cocoa powder	112 g	3¾ oz
Cream cheese	225 g	8 oz
Dates	180 g	6 oz
Flour, cake	120 g	4 oz
Flour, plain (all-purpose)	120 g	4 oz
Graham cracker crumbs	120 g	4 oz
Macadamia nuts	143 g	4¾ oz
Peanut butter	225 g	8 oz
Peanuts	142 g	4¾ oz
Pecans	120 g	4 oz
Pineapple, crushed	225 g	8 oz
Raisins	180 g	6 oz
Rolled oats	105 g	3½ oz
Sugar, dark brown	225 g	8 oz
Sugar, granulated	200 g	7 oz
Sugar, icing (confectioner's)	120 g	4 oz
Sugar, light brown	225 g	8 oz
Vegetable shortening	172 g	5¾ oz
Vegetable/corn oil	225 g	8 oz
Walnuts	120 g	4 oz

Part 1
Drinks

Take a moment to enjoy
the pure pleasure of a
hot or iced espresso drink.

Hot Coffees

Espresso

The essence of coffee and the base for all the drinks in this book. Espresso is pleasant and rich in flavour, dark in colour and crowned by hazelnut-coloured foam called crema. It is traditionally served in a demitasse.

Ingredients

Ground espresso	2 Tbsp
Water	as needed

Method

1. Using an espresso machine, extract the perfect shot within 18 to 24 seconds. One shot is equivalent to 3 Tbsp (1½ fl oz / 45 ml).

Espresso Lungo

Lungo literally means "long" in Italian, with reference to the extraction time.

Ingredients

Ground espresso	2 Tbsp
Water	as needed

Method

1. Prepared like an espresso, but with a longer extraction time that can last up to a minute. Since the ground coffee is exposed to heat longer, the result is a mild but bitter espresso with a thin film of crema.

2. In this method, more water is passed through the ground coffee, resulting in a ¼ cup (2 fl oz / 60 ml) shot.

Espresso Ristretto

Fuller in body without the bitter tones of coffee. Usually preferred by espresso coffee lovers.

Ingredients

Ground espresso	2 Tbsp
Water	as needed

Method

1. Prepared like an espresso, but with a shorter extraction time.

2. In this method, only a small amount of water is passed through the ground coffee, resulting in a fuller, bolder 2 Tbsp (1 fl oz / 30 ml) shot.

Double Espresso

Also known as *doppio* in Italian, this is in essence, two servings of espresso in a single cup.

Ingredients

Ground espresso	4 Tbsp
Water	as needed

Method

1. Using an espresso machine, extract a double shot of espresso.

Espresso Con Panna

Literally "espresso with cream" in Italian, this is a shot of espresso topped with a dollop of cream, and served in a demitasse.

Ingredients

Espresso (page 29)	1 shot (3 Tbsp)
Whipped cream	a dollop

Method

1. Using an espresso machine, extract a shot of espresso.

2. Top with a dollop of cream.

Espresso Romano

An espresso served with a twist
of lemon rind on the side.

Ingredients

Espresso (page 29)	1 shot (3 Tbsp)
Lemon rind	as desired

Method

1. Using an espresso machine, extract a
   shot of espresso.

2. Serve with lemon rind on the side.

Espresso Machiatto

A serving of espresso just marked with a touch of steamed milk. Usually topped with a little froth to distinguish it from the regular espresso.

Ingredients

Espresso (page 29)	1 shot (3 Tbsp)
Steamed milk	1 Tbsp
Froth	a dollop

Method

1. Using an espresso machine, extract a shot of espresso.

2. Add the steamed milk, then mark with some froth.

Dry Cappuccino

A serving of espresso with less steamed milk and more froth than a regular cappuccino.

Ingredients

Espresso (page 29)	1 shot (3 Tbsp)
Steamed milk	2 Tbsp
Froth	¼ cup

Method

1. Using an espresso machine, extract a shot of espresso.

2. Add the steamed milk and froth.

Wet Cappuccino

A serving of espresso with more steamed milk and less froth than a regular cappuccino.

Ingredients

Espresso (page 29)	1 shot (3 Tbsp)
Steamed milk	¼ cup
Froth	2 Tbsp

Method

1. Using an espresso machine, extract a shot of espresso.

2. Add the steamed milk and froth.

Traditional Cappuccino

A serving of espresso with equal amounts of steamed milk and froth. Traditionally served in a 6-fl oz (180-ml) cup.

Ingredients

Espresso (page 29)	1 shot (3 Tbsp)
Steamed milk	1 shot (3 Tbsp)
Froth	1 shot (3 Tbsp)

Method

1. Using an espresso machine, extract a shot of espresso.

2. Add an equal amount of steamed milk.

3. Add the same amount of froth to fill the cup.

4. Decorate as desired.

Caffè Americano

A shot of espresso diluted
with hot water.

Ingredients

Espresso (page 29)	1 shot (3 Tbsp)
Hot water	⅜ to ½ cup

Method

1. Using an espresso machine, extract a
   shot of espresso.

2. Add enough hot water to fill the cup
   three-quarters of the way.

3. Serve immediately.

Caffè Latte

A single shot of espresso with twice the amount of steamed milk and a little froth.

Ingredients

Espresso (page 29)	1 shot (3 Tbsp)
Steamed milk	⅜ to ½ cup

Method

1. Using an espresso machine, extract a shot of espresso.

2. Add enough steamed milk to fill the cup up to three-quarters full.

3. Decorate as desired.

Caffè Mocha

A serving of espresso with milk and chocolate. Frothed milk or softly whipped cream is added before serving.

Ingredients

Chocolate syrup	1 to 2 Tbsp + more for decorating
Steamed milk	¼ cup
Froth	as needed
Espresso (page 29)	1 shot (3 Tbsp)

Method

1. Pour 1 to 2 Tbsp chocolate syrup into a coffee cup.

2. Add the steamed milk, then enough froth to fill the cup.

3. Add the espresso, dribbling it slowly against the back of a spoon to create a layer of coffee.

4. To decorate, draw concentric circles with the chocolate syrup, spacing them ½-in (1-cm) apart. Using a toothpick or any pointed object, draw straight lines starting from the centre out towards the edge of the cup, cutting through the chocolate circles.

Hot Choco Macadamia Malt

A caffè mocha made more delicious with the flavours of nutty macadamia and creamy malted milk.

Ingredients

Chocolate syrup	1 Tbsp + more for decorating
Macadamia nut flavoured syrup	1 Tbsp
Malted milk powder	½ Tbsp
Espresso (page 29)	1 shot (3 Tbsp)
Steamed milk	¼ cup
Froth	as needed

Method

1. Pour the chocolate syrup into a glass.

2. Add the macadamia flavoured syrup and malted milk powder.

3. Add the shot of espresso.

4. Add the steamed milk and enough froth to fill the glass.

5. To decorate, make small drops of chocolate syrup on the froth. In one continuous motion, drag a toothpick or any pointed object down the middle of the drops.

White Chocolate Mocha

A white chocolate version of a caffè mocha.

Ingredients

White chocolate syrup	1 to 2 Tbsp
Steamed milk	¼ cup
Froth	as needed
Espresso (page 29)	1 shot (3 Tbsp)

Method

1. Pour the white chocolate syrup into a glass.

2. Add the steamed milk, then some froth.

3. Add the shot of espresso, dribbling it slowly against the back of a spoon to create a layer of coffee.

4. Add some additional froth to fill the glass.

Café Au Lait

Café au lait translates to "coffee with milk" in French. Made with strong drip brew, or in this case, a caffè Americano with steamed milk.

Ingredients

Caffè Americano (page 39) or a dark brew	⅜ to ½ cup
Steamed milk	⅜ to ½ cup

Method

1. Pour the strong coffee into a coffee cup, filling it up halfway.

2. Add the same amount of steamed milk to the cup.

3. Serve immediately.

Hot Mandarin Orange

A caffè mocha with the zesty
flavour of mandarin oranges.

Ingredients

Chocolate syrup	1 Tbsp
Mandarin orange flavoured syrup	2 Tbsp
Espresso (page 29)	1 shot (3 Tbsp)
Steamed milk	¼ cup
Froth	as needed

Method

1. Pour the syrups into a coffee cup.

2. Add the shot of espresso, followed by the steamed milk.

3. Top with enough froth to fill the cup.

Hot New York Cheesecake

An espresso drink with the creamy flavour of cheesecake and French vanilla.

Ingredients

Cheesecake flavoured syrup	1 Tbsp
French vanilla flavoured syrup	1 Tbsp
Espresso (page 29)	1 shot (3 Tbsp)
Steamed milk	¼ cup
Froth	as needed
Chocolate syrup for decorating	

Method

1. Pour the syrups into a coffee cup.

2. Add the shot of espresso.

3. Add the steamed milk and enough froth to fill the cup.

4. To decorate, make small drops of chocolate syrup on the froth. In one continuous motion, drag a toothpick or any pointed object down the middle of the drops.

Hot Tiramisu

A pick-me-up flavoured with creamy vanilla, chocolate and espresso.

Ingredients

Chocolate syrup	1 Tbsp
Tiramisu flavoured syrup	1 Tbsp
French vanilla flavoured syrup	½ Tbsp
Espresso (page 29)	1 shot (3 Tbsp)
Steamed milk	¼ cup

Garnish (as needed)

Froth

Cocoa powder

Chocolate shavings

Method

1. Pour the syrups into a coffee cup.

2. Add the shot of espresso.

3. Add the steamed milk and enough froth to fill the cup.

4. Dust with cocoa powder and garnish with chocolate shavings.

Dolce Latte

A caffè latte sweetened with condensed milk and a hint of caramel.

Ingredients

Sweetened condensed milk	1 Tbsp
Caramel flavoured syrup	½ Tbsp
Espresso (page 29)	1 shot (3 Tbsp)
Steamed milk	¼ cup
Froth	as needed
Chocolate syrup for decorating	

Method

1. Spoon the condensed milk into a coffee cup.

2. Add the caramel flavoured syrup followed by the shot of espresso.

3. Add the steamed milk and enough froth to fill the cup.

4. To decorate, draw horizontal lines with the chocolate syrup, spacing them about ¼-in (0.5-cm) apart. Using a toothpick or any pointed object, draw vertical lines up and down across the chocolate lines, spacing them about ¼-in (0.5-cm) apart.

Crème Caramel Latte

An espresso drink reminiscent of the custard tart, with the goodness of vanilla and caramel.

Ingredients

Caramel flavoured syrup	½ Tbsp
French vanilla flavoured syrup	½ Tbsp
Steamed milk	½ cup
Froth	as needed
Espresso (page 29)	1 shot (3 Tbsp)

Method

1. Pour the syrups into a coffee cup.

2. Add the steamed milk and enough froth to fill the cup.

3. Add the espresso, dribbling it slowly against the back of a spoon to create a layer of coffee.

4. Add additional froth to fill the cup.

Iced Coffees

Irish Mocha

A refreshing espresso drink
with chocolate and Irish cream.

Ingredients

Chocolate syrup	2 Tbsp
Irish cream flavoured syrup	1 Tbsp
Cold milk	¼ cup
Ice cubes	4 to 6 pieces
Espresso (page 29)	1 shot (3 Tbsp)

Garnish (as desired)
Whipped cream
Brown sugar crystals

Method

1. Pour the syrups into a glass.

2. Add the milk, followed by the ice cubes.

3. Add the espresso, dribbling it slowly into the glass against the back of a spoon to create a layer of coffee.

4. Top with whipped cream and sprinkle with brown sugar crystals.

Rocky Road

A playful concoction of espresso and chocolate topped with marshmallows and nuts.

Ingredients

Chocolate syrup	2 Tbsp + more for drizzling
Espresso (page 29)	1 shot (3 Tbsp)
Chocolate milano flavoured syrup	1 Tbsp
Cold milk	¼ cup
Ice cubes	4 to 6 pieces

Garnish (as desired)

Whipped cream

Mini marshmallows

Chopped walnuts

Chocolate syrup

Method

1. Spoon some chocolate syrup down the sides of a glass to form lines.

2. In a separate glass, stir together the espresso, 2 Tbsp chocolate syrup, chocolate milano flavoured syrup and milk.

3. Pour the mixture into the prepared glass.

4. Add the ice cubes.

5. Top with whipped cream, marshmallows and walnuts.

6. Drizzle with chocolate syrup.

Banana Nut Latte

The combined flavours of bananas and macadamia nuts provide a subtle but distinct taste to this iced coffee drink.

Ingredients

Crème de banana flavoured syrup	1 Tbsp
Macadamia nut flavoured syrup	½ Tbsp
Cold milk	½ cup
Ice cubes	4 to 6 pieces
Espresso (page 29)	1 shot (3 Tbsp)
Banana	1, peeled, sliced and drizzled with melted chocolate

Method

1. Pour the syrups into a glass.

2. Add the milk, followed by the ice cubes.

3. Add the espresso, slowly dribbling it into the glass against the back of a spoon to create a layer of coffee.

4. Garnish with chocolate-drizzled banana slices.

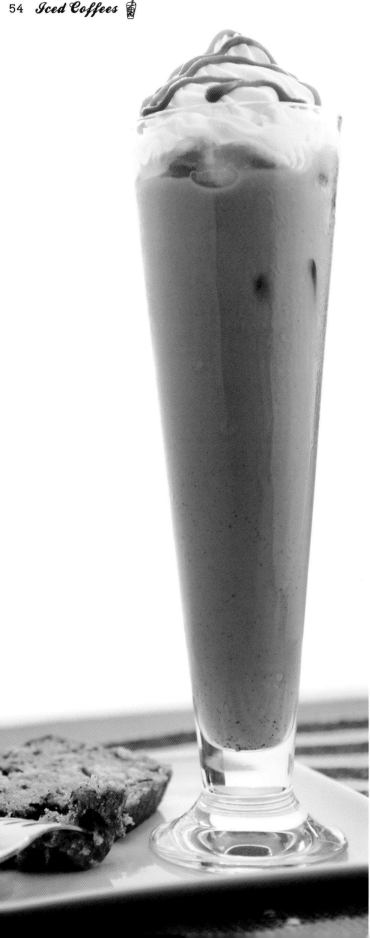

White Rabbit

Coffee made sweet and sinful
with white chocolate and caramel
flavoured syrups.

Ingredients

Espresso (page 29)	1 shot (3 Tbsp)
White chocolate syrup	2 Tbsp
Caramel flavoured syrup	1 Tbsp
Cold milk	½ cup
Ice cubes	4 to 6 pieces

Garnish (as desired)

Whipped cream

Caramel sauce

Method

1. Pour the espresso, syrups and milk into
   a tall glass. Stir well.

2. Add the ice cubes.

3. Top with whipped cream and drizzle with
   caramel sauce.

Butter Pecan and Rum Latte

A buttery and nutty espresso drink with a hint of rum.

Ingredients

Melted chocolate	1 Tbsp
Finely chopped pecans	1 Tbsp
Espresso (page 29)	1 shot (3 Tbsp)
Hazelnut flavoured syrup	1 Tbsp
Butter pecan flavoured syrup	1 Tbsp
Cold milk	½ cup
Ice cubes	4 to 6 pieces

Method

1. Line the rim of a glass with the melted chocolate, then dip it on the finely chopped pecans. Allow to dry.

2. In a separate glass, stir together the espresso and syrups.

3. Pour the milk into the prepared glass, followed by the ice cubes.

4. Add the espresso and syrup mixture, slowly dribbling it into the glass against the back of a spoon to create a layer.

Butterfinger Latte

A coffee rendition of the famous candy bar with a nutty, buttery kick.

Ingredients

Butterscotch flavoured syrup	1 Tbsp
Peanut butter flavoured syrup	1 Tbsp
Cold milk	½ cup
Ice cubes	4 to 6 pieces
Espresso (page 29)	1 shot (3 Tbsp)
Chocolate syrup	1 Tbsp

Garnish (as desired)

Whipped cream

Butterfinger candy, chopped

Method

1. Pour the butterscotch and peanut butter flavoured syrups into a cocktail glass.

2. Add the milk, followed by the ice cubes.

3. Add the espresso, dribbling it slowly into the glass against the back of a spoon to create a layer of coffee.

4. Add the chocolate syrup.

5. Top with whipped cream and chopped Butterfinger candy.

Almond Roca

An espresso drink made richer with chocolate and Almond Roca syrups. It tastes just like the famous chocolate candy!

Ingredients

Chocolate syrup	2 Tbsp
Almond Roca syrup	1 Tbsp
Cold milk	¼ cup
Ice cubes	4 to 6 pieces
Espresso (page 29)	1 shot (3 Tbsp)

Garnish (as desired)

Whipped cream

Chocolate curls

Method

1. Pour the syrups into a glass.

2. Add the milk, followed by the ice cubes.

3. Add the espresso and lightly stir the milk with the espresso, being careful not to touch the syrup layer to keep the layered effect.

4. Top with whipped cream and decorate with chocolate curls.

Dessert Coffees

Mocha Rumba

Ice-blended mocha with a kick of rum.

Ingredients

Espresso (page 29)	1 shot (3 Tbsp)
Cold milk	¼ cup
Rum flavoured syrup	1 Tbsp
Chocolate syrup	2 Tbsp
Sugar syrup (page 197)	2 Tbsp
Crushed ice	1 glass
Cocoa powder	as needed

Method

1. In a blender, process the espresso, milk, syrups and crushed ice together for 20 to 30 seconds until the mixture resembles smooth slush.

2. Pour into a tall glass.

3. Dust with cocoa powder.

Black Forest

Tastes like the popular cake named after the mountain in Germany.

Ingredients

Espresso (page 29)	1 shot (3 Tbsp)
Cold milk	¼ cup
Cherry flavoured syrup	1 Tbsp
Orgeat almond flavoured syrup	½ Tbsp
Chocolate syrup	2 Tbsp
Sugar syrup (page 197)	2 Tbsp
Chocolate ice cream	2 scoops
Crushed ice	¾ glass

Garnish (as desired)

Whipped cream

Chocolate shavings

Cocoa powder

Maraschino cherry

Method

1. In a blender, process the espresso, milk, syrups, ice cream and crushed ice for 20 to 30 seconds until the mixture resembles smooth slush.

2. Pour into a tall glass.

3. Top with whipped cream and chocolate shavings.

4. Dust with cocoa powder and top with a cherry.

Almond Coffee Freeze

A luscious blended treat with a splash of amaretto syrup and almond extract.

Ingredients

Espresso (page 29)	1 shot (3 Tbsp)
Cold milk	¼ cup
Almond extract	½ tsp
Amaretto flavoured syrup	1 Tbsp
Sugar syrup (page 197)	2 Tbsp
Vanilla ice cream	2 scoops
Crushed ice	¾ glass

Garnish (as desired)

Whipped cream

Toasted sliced almond

Dark chocolate cookie crumbs

Method

1. In a blender, process the espresso, milk, almond extract, syrups, ice cream and crushed ice for 20 to 30 seconds until the mixture resembles smooth slush.

2. Pour into a tall glass.

3. Top with whipped cream and toasted sliced almonds.

4. Sprinkle with dark chocolate cookie crumbs.

Caramel Latte

Nutty, creamy and milky—all the goodness of dessert in a coffee drink!

Ingredients

Espresso (page 29)	1 shot (3 Tbsp)
Cold milk	⅓ cup
Caramel flavoured syrup	1 Tbsp
Sugar syrup (page 197)	2 Tbsp
Vanilla ice cream	2 scoops
Crushed ice	¾ glass

Garnish (as desired)

Whipped cream

Caramel sauce

Method

1. In a blender, process the espresso, milk, syrups, ice cream and crushed ice for 20 to 30 seconds until the mixture resembles smooth slush.

2. Pour into a tall glass.

3. Garnish with whipped cream and caramel sauce.

Dark Chocolate Truffle Freeze

My personal favourite! Rich, thick and dark.

Ingredients

Espresso (page 29)	1 shot (3 Tbsp)
Cold milk	¼ cup
Chocolate milano flavoured syrup	1 Tbsp
Chocolate syrup	2 Tbsp
Sugar syrup (page 197)	2 Tbsp
Black/dark cocoa powder	1 Tbsp
Chocolate ice cream	2 scoops
Crushed ice	¾ glass

Garnish (as desired)

Whipped cream

Chocolate shavings

Method

1. In a blender, process the espresso, milk, syrups, cocoa powder, ice cream and crushed ice for 20 to 30 seconds until the mixture resembles smooth slush.

2. Pour into a tall glass.

3. Top with whipped cream and chocolate shavings.

Toffee Coffee

Just like toffee, this ice blend is creamy and buttery with a hint of nutty almonds.

Ingredients

Espresso (page 29)	1 shot (3 Tbsp)
Cold milk	¼ cup
Almond extract	½ tsp
Butterscotch sauce	1 Tbsp
Chocolate syrup	2 Tbsp
Sugar syrup (page 197)	2 Tbsp
Vanilla ice cream	2 scoops
Crushed ice	¾ glass

Garnish (as desired)

Whipped cream

Butterscotch sauce

Chocolate syrup

Toasted sliced almonds

Method

1. In a blender, process the espresso, milk, almond extract, butterscotch sauce, syrups, ice cream and crushed ice for 20 to 30 seconds until the mixture resembles smooth slush.

2. Pour into a tall glass.

3. Top with whipped cream and drizzle with butterscotch sauce and chocolate syrup. Sprinkle with toasted sliced almonds.

Macadamia Coconut Blast

All the flavours of Hawaii! The perfect combination of coconut and macadamia nuts enhances the taste of the espresso.

Ingredients

Espresso (page 29)	1 shot (3 Tbsp)
Cold milk	¼ cup
Macadamia nut flavoured syrup	½ Tbsp
Coconut flavoured syrup	1 Tbsp
Sugar syrup (page 197)	2 Tbsp
Crushed ice	1 glass

Garnish (as desired)

Whipped cream

Toasted coconut flakes

Method

1. In a blender, process the espresso, milk, syrups and crushed ice for 20 to 30 seconds until the mixture resembles smooth slush.

2. Pour into a tall glass

3. Top with whipped cream and toasted coconut flakes.

Wild Cherry

Go wild with this espresso treat flavoured with sweet cherry and creamy vanilla ice cream!

Ingredients

Espresso (page 29)	1 shot (3 Tbsp)
Cold milk	¼ cup
Cherry flavoured syrup	1 Tbsp
Grenadine syrup	1 tsp
Sugar syrup (page 197)	2 Tbsp
Vanilla ice cream	2 scoops
Crushed ice	¾ glass

Garnish (as desired)

Whipped cream
Red candy sprinkles
Maraschino cherry

Method

1. In a blender, process the espresso, milk, syrups, ice cream and crushed ice for 20 to 30 seconds until the mixture resembles smooth slush.

2. Pour into a tall glass.

3. Top with whipped cream and red candy sprinkles. Finish with a cherry.

Mint Chocolate Chip Blast

A minty and chocolaty coffee drink made richer with vanilla ice cream.

Ingredients

Espresso (page 29)	1 shot (3 Tbsp)
Cold milk	¼ cup
Peppermint flavoured syrup	1 Tbsp
Chocolate syrup	2 Tbsp
Sugar syrup (page 197)	2 Tbsp
Vanilla ice cream	2 scoops
Crushed ice	¾ glass

Garnish (as desired)

Whipped cream

Chocolate mint candy, chopped

Method

1. In a blender, process the espresso, milk, syrups, ice cream and crushed ice for 20 to 30 seconds until the mixture resembles smooth slush.

2. Pour into a tall glass.

3. Top with whipped cream and chocolate mint candy.

Mudslide Mocha

A refreshing blend of espresso and chocolate syrup with speckles of dark chocolate cookie.

Ingredients

Espresso (page 29)	1 shot (3 Tbsp)
Cold milk	¼ cup
Chocolate syrup	2 Tbsp
Sugar syrup (page 197)	2 Tbsp
Vanilla ice cream	2 scoops
Crushed ice	¾ glass
Dark chocolate sandwich cookies	2 pieces, filling removed

Garnish (as desired)

Whipped cream

Dark chocolate cookie crumbs

Miniature dark chocolate sandwich cookie

Method

1. In a blender, process the espresso, milk, syrups, ice cream and crushed ice for 20 to 30 seconds until the mixture resembles smooth slush.

2. Add the dark chocolate cookies and pulse the blender 5 to 10 times.

3. Pour into a tall glass.

4. Top with whipped cream and dark chocolate cookie crumbs. Finish with a miniature dark chocolate sandwich cookie.

Cotton Candy

An espresso drink flavoured with the all-time favourite kiddie treat of coloured candy sprinkles, and thickened with vanilla ice cream.

Ingredients

Espresso (page 29)	1 shot (3 Tbsp)
Cold milk	¼ cup
Strawberry flavoured syrup	1 Tbsp
Vanilla flavoured syrup	½ Tbsp
Sugar syrup (page 197)	2 Tbsp
Vanilla ice cream	2 scoops
Crushed ice	¾ glass

Garnish (as desired)
Whipped cream
Coloured candy sprinkles

Method

1. In a blender, process the espresso, milk, syrups, ice cream and crushed ice for 20 to 30 seconds until the mixture resembles smooth slush.

2. Pour into a tall glass.

3. Top with whipped cream and coloured candy sprinkles.

Banana Split Mocha

Espresso with a blast of chocolate, vanilla and strawberry. It has all the flavours of the famous ice cream dessert and tastes almost like a milkshake.

Ingredients

Espresso (page 29)	1 shot (3 Tbsp)
Cold milk	¼ cup
Crème de banana flavoured syrup	1 tsp
Strawberry flavoured syrup	1 tsp
Chocolate syrup	2 Tbsp
Sugar syrup (page 197)	2 Tbsp
Vanilla ice cream	2 scoops
Crushed ice	¾ glass

Garnish (as desired)

Whipped cream

Chopped walnuts

Chocolate syrup

Maraschino cherry

Method

1. In a blender, process the espresso, milk, syrups, ice cream and crushed ice for 20 to 30 seconds until the mixture resembles smooth slush.

2. Pour into a tall glass.

3. Top with whipped cream and chopped walnuts. Drizzle with chocolate syrup, then finish with a cherry.

Cocktail Coffees

Candy Cane

A festive mix of espresso, strawberry flavoured syrup, crème de menthe and whipped cream. Great for the holidays!

Ingredients

Crème de menthe	1 Tbsp
Strawberry flavoured syrup	2 Tbsp
Espresso (page 29)	1 shot (3 Tbsp)
Ice cubes	as needed

Garnish

Whipped cream	a dollop
Mint flavoured candy cane	1

Method

1. Pour the crème de menthe into a tall glass.
2. Add the strawberry flavoured syrup.
3. Add the espresso.
4. Add some ice cubes, filling the glass three-quarters of the way.
5. Top with a dollop of whipped cream and garnish with a mint flavoured candy cane.

Café Frangelico

Espresso spruced up with hazelnut liqueur, coffee liqueur and whipped cream. The distinct hazelnut flavour of this cocktail is unmistakably North Italian.

Ingredients

Coffee liqueur	2 Tbsp
Liquid (whipping) cream	2 Tbsp
Ice cubes	as needed
Hazelnut liqueur	1 shot (3 Tbsp)
Espresso (page 29)	1 shot (3 Tbsp)

Method

1. Pour the coffee liqueur into a rocks glass (a short glass tumbler).

2. Add the liquid cream.

3. Add some ice cubes, filling the glass halfway.

4. Add the hazelnut liqueur.

5. Add the espresso, slowly dribbling it into the glass against the back of a spoon to create a layer of coffee.

Café Amaretto

A coffee cocktail made irresistible with the fragrance and flavour of almonds.

Ingredients

Coffee liqueur	1 Tbsp
Amaretto liqueur	1 shot (3 Tbsp)
Espresso (page 29)	1 shot (3 Tbsp)
Ice cubes	as needed

Garnish

Whipped cream	a dollop
Maraschino cherry	1

Method

1. Pour the coffee and amaretto liqueurs and espresso into a cocktail glass.

2. Add some ice cubes, filling the glass three-quarters of the way.

3. Top with a dollop of cream and garnish with a cherry.

Irish Kiss

A lovely after-dinner drink.

Ingredients

Coffee liqueur	2 Tbsp
Amaretto liqueur	2 Tbsp
Ice cubes	as needed
Irish cream liqueur	2 Tbsp
Espresso (page 29)	1 shot (3 Tbsp)

Method

1. Pour the coffee liqueur into a rocks glass (a short glass tumbler).

2. Add the amaretto liqueur.

3. Add some ice cubes, filling the glass halfway.

4. Add the Irish cream liqueur.

5. Add the espresso, slowly dribbling it into the glass against the back of a spoon to create a layer of coffee.

Espresso Martini

This delicious cocktail is a good mix
of caffeine and alcohol.

Ingredients

Ice cubes	as needed
Espresso (page 29)	2 Tbsp
Coffee liqueur	2 Tbsp
Vodka	1 shot (3 Tbsp)
Irish cream liqueur	2 Tbsp

Method

1. In a cocktail shaker, place some ice cubes
   and all the other ingredients, and shake it
   for about 10 seconds.

2. Strain the drink into a martini glass and
   serve.

Espresso A' Lorange

A bold yet refreshing drink. Salut!

Ingredients

Orange liqueur	2 Tbsp
Cognac	2 Tbsp
Ice cubes	as needed
Espresso (page 29)	1 shot (3 Tbsp)
Orange rind	as desired

Method

1. Pour the orange liqueur into a rocks glass (a short glass tumbler).

2. Add the cognac.

3. Add some ice cubes, filling the glass halfway.

4. Add the espresso, slowly dribbling it into the glass against the back of a spoon to create a layer of coffee.

5. Garnish with orange rind.

Espresso Mojito

The famous Cuban drink is made bolder with a shot of espresso in this recipe.

Ingredients

Mint leaves	1 Tbsp + more for garnish
Sugar	1 Tbsp
Crème de menthe	½ Tbsp
Dark rum	1 shot (3 Tbsp)
Espresso (page 29)	1 shot (3 Tbsp)
Ice cubes	as needed
Club soda	a splash

Method

1. Place the mint leaves and sugar in a tall glass.

2. Crush the mint leaves with the sugar using a muddler until the juices are released.

3. Add the crème de menthe, rum and espresso.

4. Add enough ice cubes to fill the glass three-quarters of the way.

5. Add a splash of club soda.

6. Garnish with mint leaves.

Creamsicle

This recipe is inspired by the creamsicle, a popsicle where vanilla ice cream is coated with a layer of sorbet, with an extra kick from a shot of espresso!

Ingredients

White chocolate sauce	2 Tbsp
Orange liqueur	2 Tbsp
Ice cubes	as needed
Espresso (page 29)	1 shot (3 Tbsp)

Garnish

Whipped cream	a dollop
Orange	1 slice

Method

1. Pour the white chocolate sauce into a tall glass.

2. Add the orange liqueur.

3. Add some ice cubes, filling the glass halfway.

4. Add the espresso, slowly dribbling it into the glass against the back of a spoon to create a layer of coffee.

5. Top with a dollop of whipped cream and garnish with a slice of orange.

White Russian Espresso

Feel like royalty with this smooth and elegant drink.

Ingredients

Coffee liqueur	2 Tbsp
Vodka	1 shot (3 Tbsp)
Liquid (whipping) cream	1 shot (3 Tbsp)
Ice cubes	as needed
Espresso (page 29)	1 shot (3 Tbsp)

Method

1. Pour the coffee liqueur into a rocks glass (a short glass tumbler).

2. Add the vodka and liquid cream.

3. Add some ice cubes, filling the glass halfway.

4. Add the espresso, slowly dribbling it into the glass against the back of a spoon to create a layer of coffee.

Cappuccino Martini

This cocktail was inspired by a dear friend's gift of Godiva cappuccino liqueur. Cheers!

Ingredients

Chocolate malt powder	as needed
Ice cubes	as needed
Espresso (page 29)	1 shot (3 Tbsp)
Cappuccino liqueur	1 Tbsp
Vodka	1 shot (3 Tbsp)
Light cream (half-and-half)	1 Tbsp
Sugar syrup (page 197)	1 Tbsp

Method

1. Line the rim of a martini glass with some chocolate malt powder.

2. In a cocktail shaker, place some ice cubes, the espresso, cappuccino liqueur, vodka, light cream and sugar syrup, and shake it for about 10 seconds.

3. Strain the drink into the prepared martini glass and serve.

Part 2
Desserts

Savour each bite with
an espresso drink.

Cookies

Chocolate Chip Cookies

One of my best-kept secrets, until now! There are thousands of recipes for such cookies, but after several experiments, this is my favourite. Enjoy!

Makes about 36 cookies

Ingredients

Butter	1 cup
Sugar	1 cup
Dark brown sugar	1 cup
Eggs	2
Vanilla extract	1 tsp
Plain (all-purpose) flour	2⅔ cups
Baking soda	1 tsp
Salt	1 tsp
Semi-sweet chocolate chips	2 cups

Method

1. In a mixing bowl, beat together the butter and sugars.

2. Add the eggs one at a time until completely blended.

3. Mix in the vanilla extract.

4. In a separate bowl, whisk together the flour, baking soda and salt. Gradually add the flour mixture to the butter mixture and mix until just combined.

5. Fold in the chocolate chips.

6. Place the dough in an airtight container and refrigerate for at least 1 hour or overnight.

7. Preheat the oven to 375°F (190°C). Remove the dough from the refrigerator and thaw at room temperature for 15 to 20 minutes.

8. Line several baking sheets with parchment paper.

9. Using a small (2 Tbsp / 1 oz) ice cream scoop, spoon the dough onto lined baking sheets, spacing them about 2 in (5 cm) apart.

10. Bake for 9 to 12 minutes, or until the edges are slightly golden and the centre is still slightly soft.

11. Allow to cool for about 5 minutes before serving. Store in an airtight container at room temperature for up to 4 days.

White Chocolate Macadamia Cookies

I first tried these cookies as a student in California Culinary Academy. These cookies were a staple in many cafés in California then. Use Callebaut white chocolate if you can get your hands on some.

Makes about 30 cookies

Ingredients

Butter	1 cup
Sugar	½ cup
Brown sugar	1½ cups
Eggs	2
Vanilla extract	1 tsp
Light corn syrup	1 Tbsp
Plain (all-purpose) flour	3 cups
Baking soda	1 tsp
Salt	1 tsp
White chocolate	1¾ cups, chopped
Macadamia nuts	1½ cups, chopped

Method

1. Using an electric mixer, beat the butter and sugars on low speed until combined.

2. Add the eggs one at a time.

3. Mix in the vanilla extract and light corn syrup.

4. In a separate bowl, whisk together the flour, baking soda and salt. Gradually add to the butter mixture, mixing until just combined.

5. Fold in the chocolate and macadamia nuts.

6. Cover and refrigerate the dough for at least 1 hour or overnight.

7. Preheat the oven to 375°F (190°C). Line several baking sheets with parchment paper.

8. Using a small (2 Tbsp / 1 oz) ice cream scoop, spoon the dough onto the lined baking sheets, spacing them about 2 in (5 cm) apart.

9. Bake for 9 to 11 minutes or until golden. The centre of the cookies should still be slightly soft.

10. Transfer the cookies to a wire rack to cool before serving. Store in an airtight container at room temperature for up to 4 days.

Chocolate Crinkles

A favourite Christmas giveaway, these cookies have a crunchy exterior and a moist centre. They start out as balls rolled in powdered sugar and end up as chocolaty treats with cracked tops.

Makes about 36 cookies

Ingredients

Vegetable oil	½ cup
Sugar	1¼ cups
Eggs	3
Vanilla extract	1 tsp
Plain (all-purpose) flour	2 cups
Cocoa powder	½ cup
Baking soda	1 tsp
Icing (confectioner's) sugar	1 cup

Method

1. Using an electric mixer, combine the oil and sugar.

2. Mix in the eggs and vanilla extract.

3. In a separate bowl, whisk together the flour, cocoa powder and baking soda. Gradually add to the liquid mixture and mix until just combined.

4. Cover and refrigerate the dough for at least 1 hour or until firm.

5. Preheat the oven to 350°F (180°C). Line several baking sheets with parchment paper.

6. Shape the dough into ¾-in (1.5-cm) balls. Roll them in icing sugar, coating them completely.

7. Place the balls on the lined baking sheets, spacing them about 2 in (5 cm) apart.

8. Bake for 10 to 12 minutes, or until the cookies are puffed and cracked on top. The cookies should look undone and be soft in the centre. The internal heat will cook them while they cool down. This will keep them crisp on the outside and moist and chewy on the inside.

9. Leave to cool completely before serving. Store in an airtight container at room temperature for up to 4 days.

Sugar Cookies

The dough allows you to make cookies in infinite shapes and sizes. Dipping them in coloured royal icing makes them even more fun.

Makes about 50 cookies

Ingredients

Butter	½ cup
Sugar	1 cup
Egg	1
Vanilla extract	1 tsp
Salt	¼ tsp
Plain (all-purpose) flour	2 cups
Baking powder	½ tsp
Ground cinnamon	¼ tsp

Icing

Icing (confectioner's) sugar	4 cups
Egg whites	2
Food colouring	as desired

Method

1. Using an electric mixer, beat the butter and sugar on medium speed until fluffy.

2. Mix in the egg and vanilla extract.

3. In a separate bowl, sift together the flour, salt, baking powder and cinnamon. Gradually add to the butter mixture, beating on low speed until a dough forms.

4. Flatten the dough into a disc and cover with plastic wrap. Refrigerate for 1 hour.

5. Line several baking sheets with parchment paper and set aside until ready to use.

6. Line a work surface with parchment paper and lightly dust with flour. Roll out the chilled dough to ¼-in (0.5-cm) thickness. Dust and flour as necessary to keep the dough from sticking. Place the dough on a cookie sheet and chill in the freezer for 15 minutes.

7. Preheat the oven to 325°F (160°C).

8. Remove the dough from the freezer and cut immediately using assorted cutters. Place the shapes on baking sheets.

9. Bake for 15 to 20 minutes or until the cookies are slightly golden at the edges, rotating the tray halfway through baking. Leave the cookies to cool completely on wire racks before decorating.

10. Prepare the icing. Mix the icing sugar and egg whites on low speed for 5 to 8 minutes. Dip the tip of a toothpick in some food colouring and mix into the icing until the desired colour is achieved.

11. To decorate, dip one side of the cookie in icing. Scrape off any excess and smoothen. Leave the icing to set slightly before decorating with accents and frills.

12. Allow to dry completely before serving. Store in an airtight container at room temperature for up to 4 days.

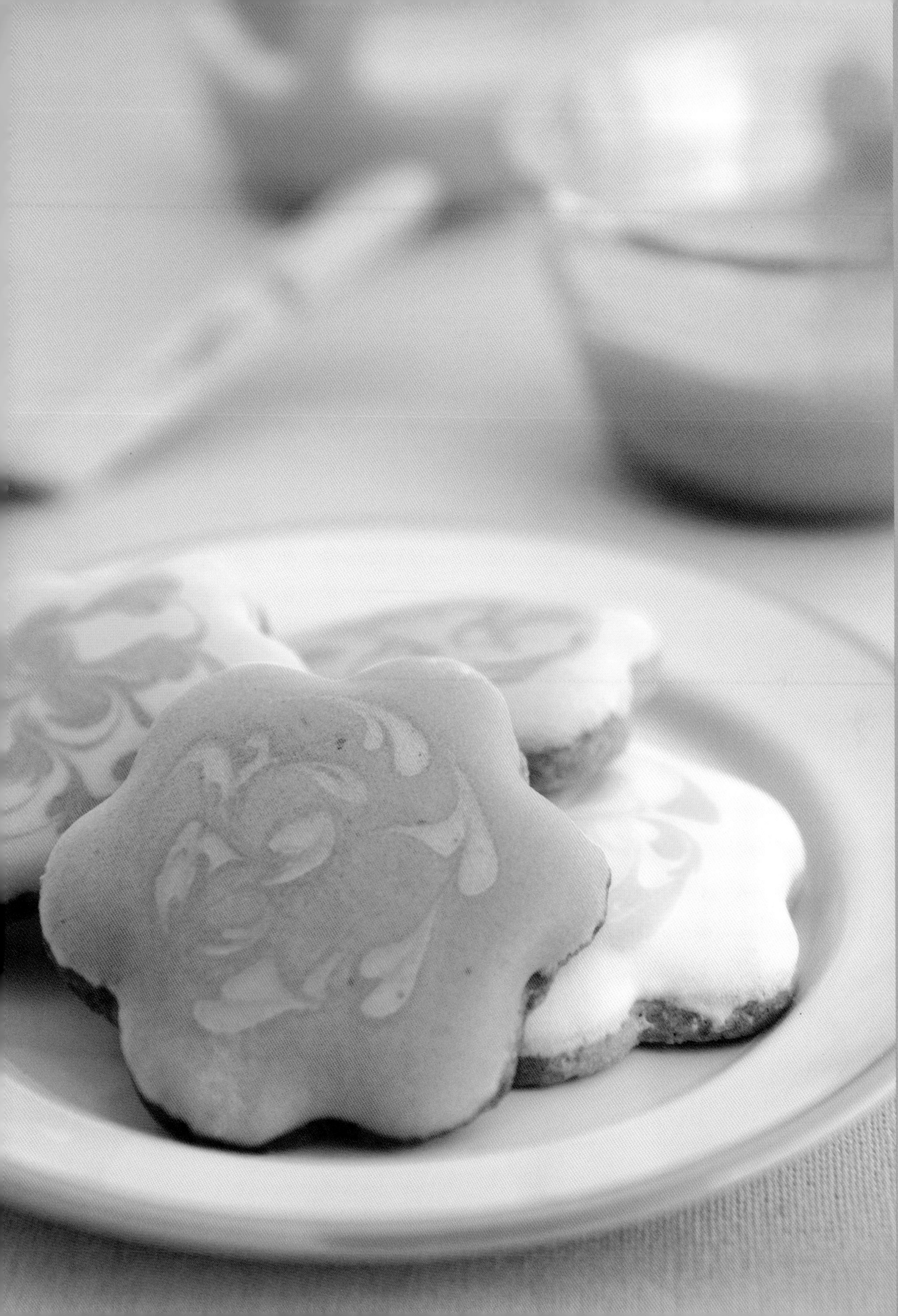

Almond Biscotti

Light and crisp, these are best enjoyed with a hot cup of coffee.

Makes about 24 slices

Ingredients

Whole almonds	¾ cup
Butter	½ cup
Sugar	¾ cup
Eggs	2, large
Orange extract	2 tsp
Orange rind	from 1 orange
Almond extract	2 tsp
Plain (all-purpose) flour	3 cups
Salt	½ tsp
Baking powder	2 tsp
Bread crumbs	½ cup

Method

1. Preheat the oven to 325°F (160°C).

2. Place the almonds on a baking sheet and bake for 5 to 10 minutes until golden. Allow to cool.

3. Using an electric mixer, cream the butter and sugar until fluffy.

4. Mix in the eggs, orange extract, orange rind and almond extract.

5. In a separate bowl, whisk together the flour, salt, baking powder and bread crumbs. Gradually add to the butter mixture.

6. Fold the almonds into the dough.

7. Transfer the dough to a lightly floured work surface. Knead until smooth and not too sticky.

8. Shape the dough into a log, 6-in (15-cm) wide and 1-in (2.5-cm) thick. Stretch the dough to fit the baking sheet, about 12 to 16 in (30 to 40 cm).

9. Bake for 35 to 40 minutes or until golden around the edges.

10. Allow to cool slightly, then slice into ½-in (1-cm) thick slices using a large, sharp knife.

11. Place the slices flat on a baking sheet and bake for another 15 to 20 minutes until golden brown.

12. Transfer to a wire rack to cool before serving. Store in an airtight container at room temperature for up to 7 days.

Peanut Butter Cookies

Turn your favourite bottled spread into these chewy cookies. Throw in some chunky peanuts for added flavour and texture.

Makes about 24 cookies

Ingredients

Butter	⅔ cup, cubed and softened
Sugar	½ cup
Brown sugar	1 cup
Peanut butter	½ cup
Egg	1
Vanilla extract	1 tsp
Plain (all-purpose) flour	1⅔ cups
Baking soda	1 tsp
Salt	½ tsp
Peanuts	1 cup, roughly chopped

Method

1. Preheat the oven to 350°F (180°C).

2. Line several baking sheets with parchment paper.

3. Using an electric mixer, mix together the butter and sugars until light and fluffy.

4. Mix in the peanut butter.

5. Mix in the egg and vanilla extract. Reduce the speed to low.

6. In a separate bowl, sift together the flour, baking soda and salt. Gradually fold into the butter mixture.

7. Add the peanuts, mixing until just combined.

8. Using a small (2 Tbsp / 1 oz) ice cream scoop, spoon the dough onto the lined baking sheets, spacing them about 2 in (5 cm) apart.

9. Bake for 8 to 10 minutes, rotating the sheets halfway through baking. The cookies should look crackly but be soft in the centre.

10. Allow to cool for 5 minutes before transferring to wire racks to cool completely before serving. Store in an airtight container at room temperature for up to 3 days.

Raspberry Sandwich Cookies

Buttery cookies filled with sweet raspberry jam, these delightful treats are best assembled right before serving.

Makes about 10 sandwich cookies

Ingredients

Butter	¾ cup, cubed
Sugar	1¼ cups
Egg	1
Vanilla extract	1 tsp
Plain (all-purpose) flour	1⅔ cups
Baking soda	1 tsp
Salt	¼ tsp
Raspberry jam	1 cup

Method

1. Preheat the oven to 350°F (180°C).

2. Line several baking sheets with parchment paper.

3. Using an electric mixer, beat the butter and sugar on medium speed until light and fluffy.

4. Mix in the egg and vanilla extract.

5. In a separate bowl, whisk together the flour, baking soda and salt. Gradually add to the butter mixture, mixing on low speed until smooth.

6. Using a small (2 Tbsp / 1 oz) ice cream scoop, spoon the dough onto the lined baking sheets, spacing them slightly apart.

7. Bake for 8 to 10 minutes, or until the cookies are golden.

8. Place on a wire rack to cool.

9. To assemble, spread about 1 Tbsp raspberry jam onto a cookie, then sandwich with another cookie. Repeat until the cookies are used up.

10. Serve or store in an airtight container at room temperature for up to 3 days.

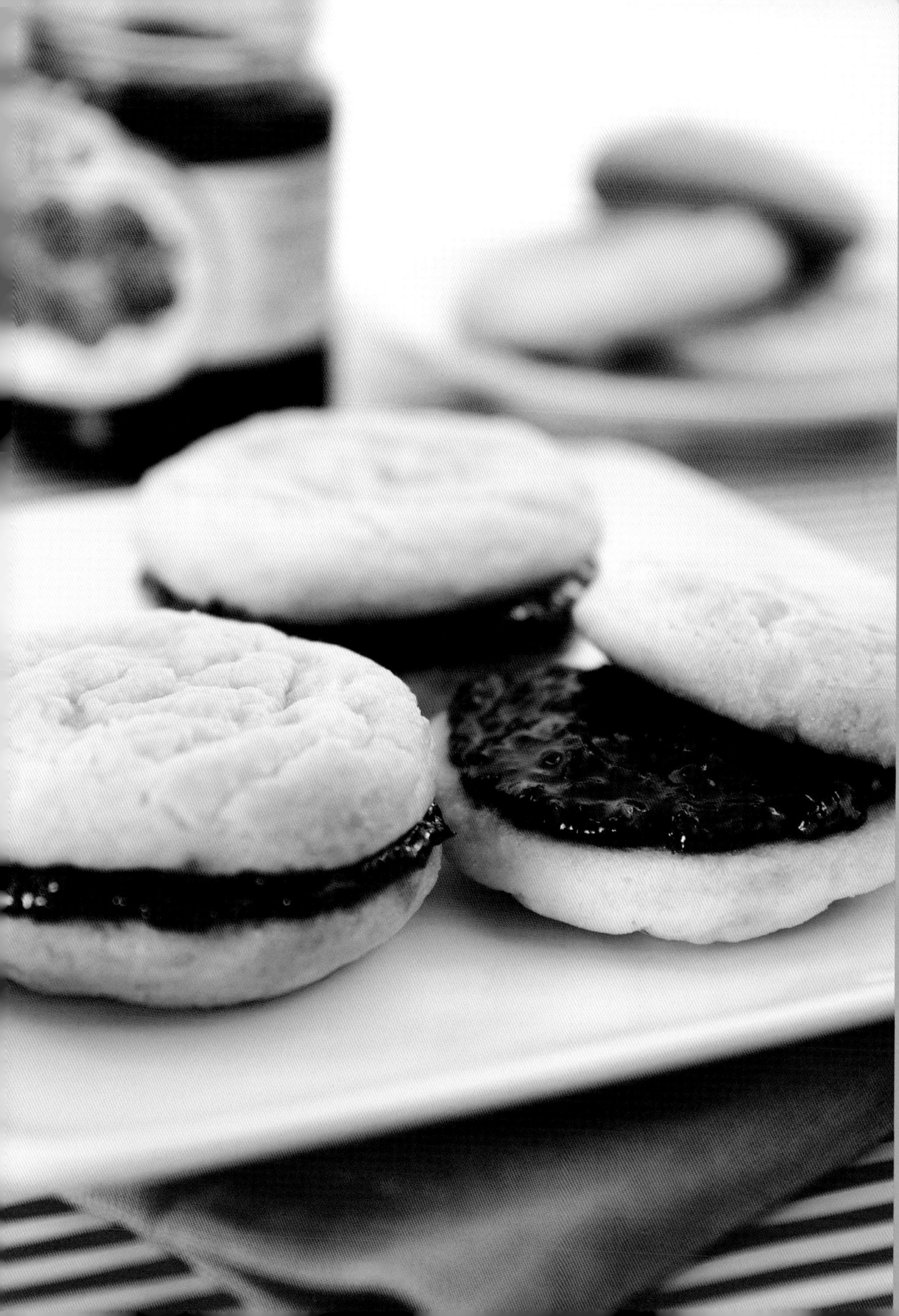

Oatmeal Raisin Cookies

Cookies with a crisp edge and a chewy centre. The secret to this recipe is the dark brown sugar which keeps the cookies moist and good for days.

Makes about 36 cookies

Ingredients

Butter	1 cup, cubed, at room temperature
Sugar	½ cup
Dark brown sugar	1½ cup
Eggs	2
Vanilla extract	1 Tbsp
Plain (all-purpose) flour	2 cups
Rolled oats	3 cups
Baking soda	1 tsp
Raisins	1½ cups

Method

1. Using an electric mixer, beat together the butter and sugars on medium speed until combined, about 2 minutes.

2. Mix in the eggs one at a time.

3. Mix in the vanilla extract.

4. In a separate bowl, whisk together the flour, rolled oats and baking soda. Gradually add to the butter mixture, mixing until just combined.

5. Fold in the raisins.

6. Cover and refrigerate the dough until firm, at least 1 hour.

7. Preheat the oven to 375°F (190°C).

8. Line several baking sheets with parchment paper.

9. Using a small (2 Tbsp / 1 oz) ice cream scoop, spoon the dough onto the lined baking sheets, spacing them about 2½ in (6 cm) apart.

10. Bake for 9 to 12 minutes or until golden brown but still soft in the centre.

11. Transfer to a wire rack to cool before serving. Store in an airtight container at room temperature for up to 4 days.

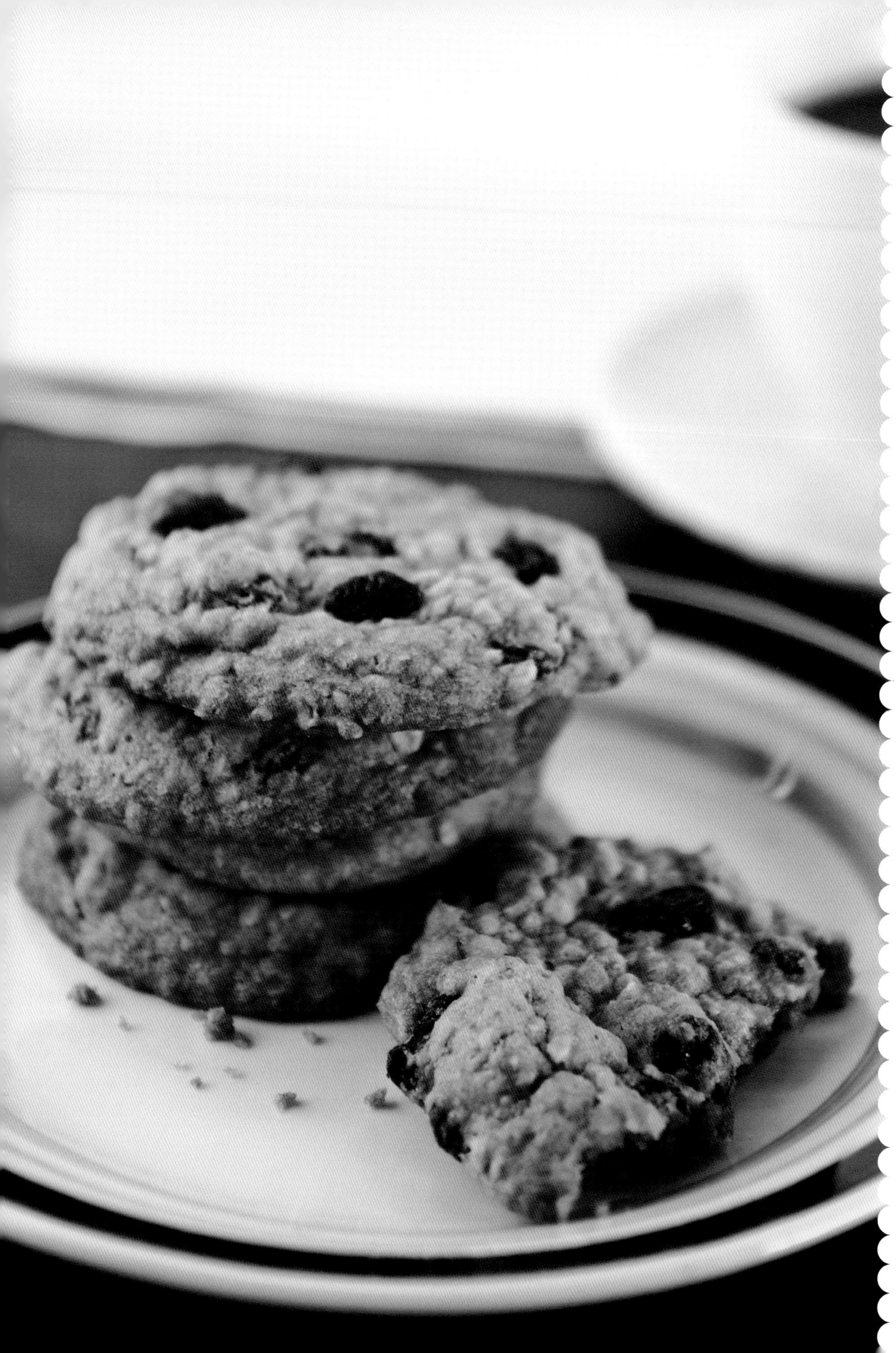

Deep Dark Chocolate Cookies

An indulgent treat for all you chocoholics! This is the ultimate dark chocolate cookie, made richer with dark chocolate chunks.

Makes about 30 cookies

Ingredients

Bittersweet chocolate	1¼ cups; ½ cup finely chopped, ¾ cup cut into chunks
Butter	½ cup, cubed
Sugar	1¼ cups
Eggs	2
Vanilla extract	1 tsp
Plain (all-purpose) flour	1 cup
Cocoa powder	½ cup
Baking soda	½ tsp
Salt	½ tsp

Method

1. In a double boiler, melt together the finely chopped chocolate and butter.

2. Using an electric mixer, beat together the sugar, eggs and vanilla extract on medium speed until combined.

3. Reduce the speed to low and add the melted chocolate mixture.

4. In another bowl, whisk together the flour, cocoa powder, baking soda and salt. Gradually add to the chocolate mixture, mixing until smooth.

5. Fold in the chocolate chunks.

6. If the dough is too soft, cover and refrigerate for at least 1 hour.

7. Preheat the oven to 350°F (180°C). Line several baking sheets with parchment paper.

8. Using a small (2 Tbsp / 1 oz) ice cream scoop, spoon the dough onto the lined baking sheets, spacing them about 2 in (5 cm) apart.

9. Bake for 10 to 12 minutes or until the cookies are crackly in appearance but still soft in the centre. Rotate the sheets halfway through baking.

10. Allow the cookies to cool on the sheets for about 10 minutes.

11. Transfer to a wire rack to cool completely before serving. Store in an airtight container at room temperature for up to 3 days.

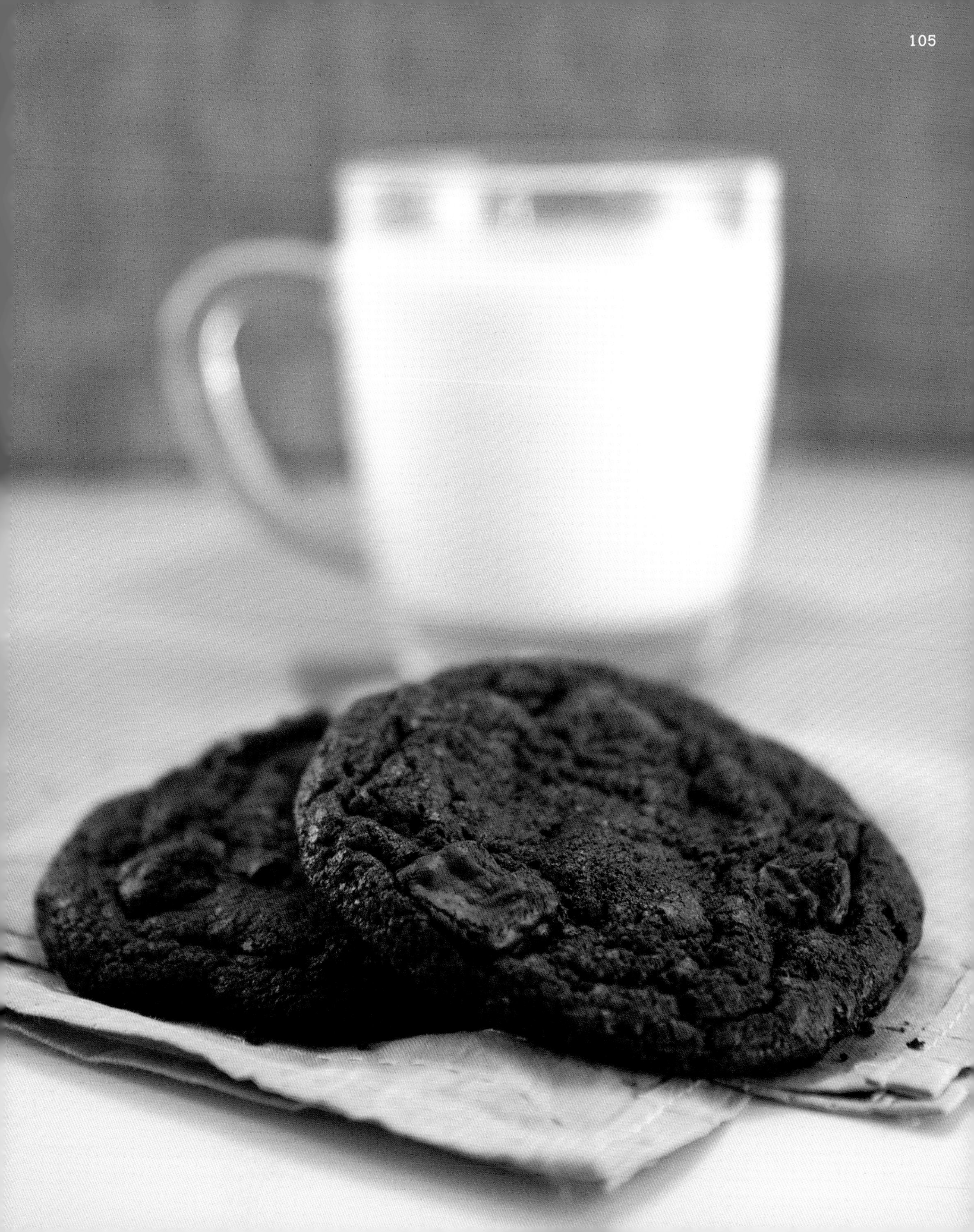

Pecan Lace Cookies

WARNING: These crisp, buttery, delicate, melt-in-your-mouth cookies are easily addictive! No worries though, as they are just as easy to prepare!

Makes about 24 cookies

Ingredients

Butter	⅓ cup, melted
Light corn syrup	2 Tbsp
Liquid (whipping) cream	2 Tbsp
Vanilla extract	1 tsp
Plain (all-purpose) flour	½ cup
Baking soda	½ tsp
Sugar	½ cup
Pecans	½ cup, finely chopped

Method

1. Preheat the oven to 375°F (190°C).

2. Grease several baking sheets.

3. Using an electric mixer, combine the butter, light corn syrup, cream and vanilla extract.

4. In a separate bowl, whisk together the flour, baking soda, sugar and finely chopped pecans. Add to the butter mixture, mixing until smooth.

5. Scoop up 1 Tbsp dough and form into a ball. Place on the greased baking sheet. Repeat to make more cookies, spacing them about 3 in (8 cm) apart. The dough will spread as it bakes.

6. Bake for 6 to 8 minutes until the cookies are golden.

7. Allow the cookies to cool on the baking sheet. If the cookies are still slightly soft in the centre, return them to the oven for another 1 to 2 minutes to make them crisp.

8. Serve or store in an airtight container at room temperature for up to 3 days.

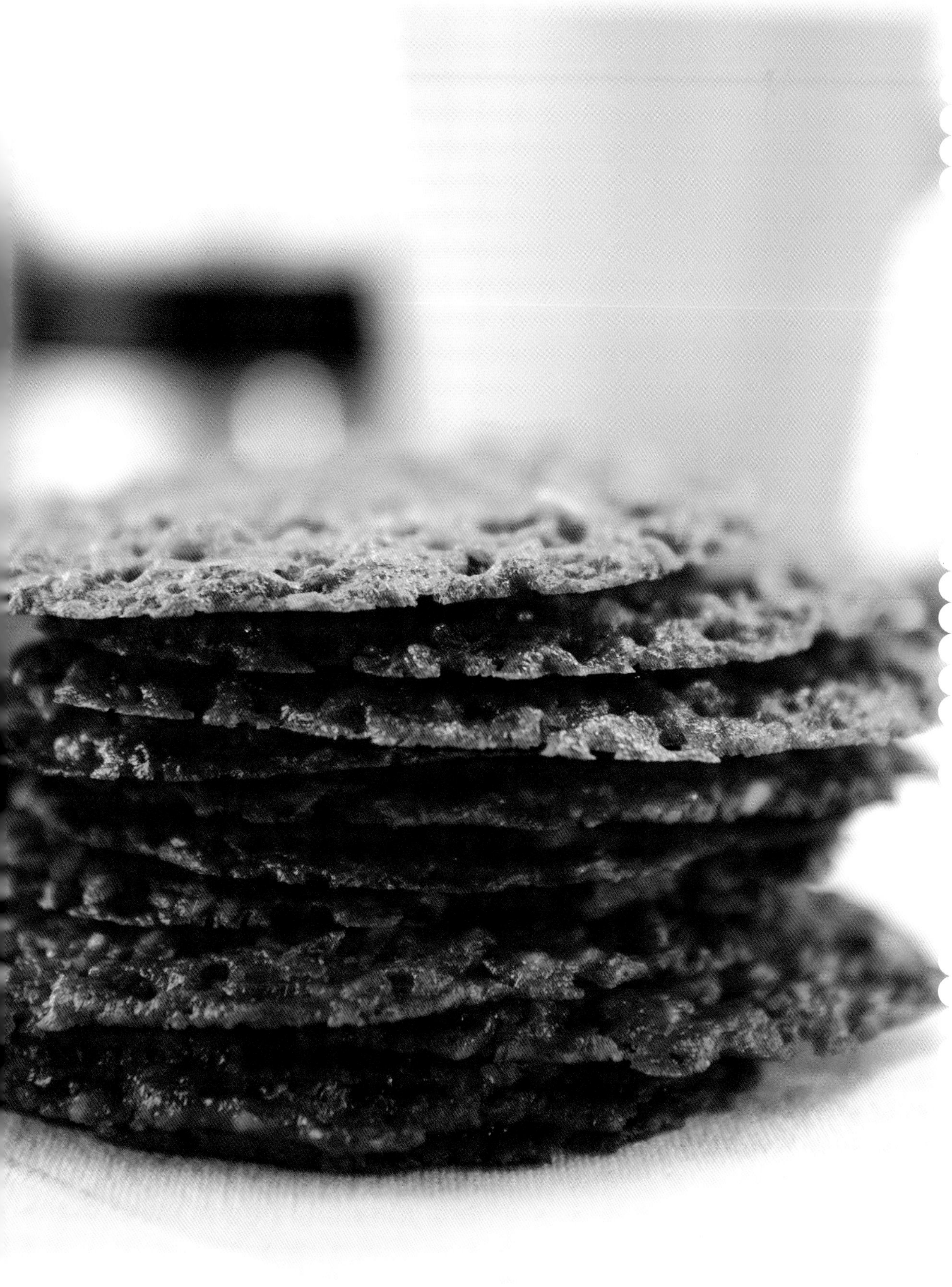

Brownies
and Bars

Lemon Squares

This is one of the most widespread and well-loved versions of this recipe. Make sure to pre-bake the crust for a crisp and flaky texture.

Makes 24 bars

Ingredients

Butter	1 cup, cubed
Icing (confectioner's) sugar	½ cup
Plain (all-purpose) flour	2 cups

Filling

Eggs	4
Sugar	1¼ cups
Lemon juice	⅓ cup
Lemon rind	1 Tbsp, grated
Plain (all-purpose) flour	4 Tbsp
Baking powder	1 tsp

Method

1. Preheat the oven to 350°F (180°C).

2. Grease and line an 8 x 12-in (20 x 30-cm) baking pan.

3. Prepare the crust. In a food processor, combine the butter and icing sugar, pulsing until the mixture resembles coarse meal. Pulse a few more times until it just forms into a ball.

4. Press the dough into the prepared pan. Bake for 15 to 20 minutes until golden.

5. Prepare the filling. Using an electric mixer, beat together the eggs and sugar until light in colour. Add the lemon juice and rind, flour and baking powder, mixing on low speed.

6. Pour the mixture over the crust and bake for 20 minutes.

7. Turn off the heat. Leave the bar in the oven for 10 minutes.

8. Cut into 2 x 2-in (5 x 5-cm) squares. Dust with icing sugar.

9. Serve or store in an airtight container at room temperature for up to 2 days. Keep refrigerated for a longer shelf life.

Zebra Brownies

The richness of these brownies goes well with the lighter taste of the cream cheese. If the playful design doesn't entice you to eat one, the delicious flavour will!

Makes 16 bars

Ingredients

Cream Cheese Batter

Cream cheese	¼ cup, softened
Butter	2 Tbsp
Sugar	2 Tbsp
Egg	1
Vanilla extract	½ tsp
Plain (all-purpose) flour	1 Tbsp

Brownie Batter

Butter	1 cup, melted
Semi-sweet chocolate	⅔ cup, chopped
Cocoa powder	½ cup
Sugar	1 cup
Eggs	4
Vanilla extract	1 tsp
Plain (all-purpose) flour	1 cup

Method

1. Preheat the oven to 350°F (180°C). Line an 8 x 8-in (20 x 20-cm) baking pan with parchment paper, leaving a 2-in (5-cm) overhang all around. Butter the base and sides.

2. Prepare the cream cheese batter. Using an electric mixer, mix together the cream cheese, butter and sugar until creamy. Mix in the egg, vanilla extract and flour. Set aside until ready to use.

3. Meanwhile, prepare the brownie batter. Combine the butter, chocolate and cocoa powder in a heatproof bowl set over a pot of simmering water. Stir occasionally until melted and smooth. Remove from the heat.

4. In a separate bowl, gradually whisk together the sugar, eggs and vanilla extract until the sugar is melted. Whisk in the chocolate mixture.

5. Gradually add in the flour, whisking just until smooth. Do not over-whisk.

6. Transfer the brownie batter into the prepared pan.

7. Place the cream cheese batter in a piping bag fitted with a round tip. Pipe lines onto the batter, about 1-in (2.5-cm) apart. Use a toothpick to create a design by drawing lines cross-wise, 1-in (2.5-cm) apart, alternately going up and down.

8. Bake for 30 to 35 minutes or until a cake tester or skewer inserted into the centre of the cake comes out slightly moist. Do not over-bake.

9. Cool completely before slicing into 2 x 2-in (5 x 5-cm) squares.

10. Serve or store in an airtight container at room temperature for up to 2 days. Keep refrigerated for a longer shelf life.

Best Gooey Brownies

I have tried many different recipes for this, but there was always something missing. Now I have finally found the right proportions for the ingredients! The key to making the perfect gooey brownies is to under-bake them. Take them out of the oven right before they are really done.

Makes 16 bars

Ingredients

Butter	¾ cup
Unsweetened chocolate	¾ cup, chopped
Sugar	1¾ cups
Eggs	3
Vanilla extract	2 tsp
Plain (all-purpose) flour	1 cup
Salt	¼ tsp

Method

1. Preheat the oven to 350°F (180°C). Lightly grease an 8 x 8-in (20 x 20-cm) baking pan.

2. In a medium bowl set over a pot of simmering water, combine the butter and chocolate, stirring occasionally until completely melted. Remove from the heat.

3. In a separate bowl, whisk the sugar into the chocolate mixture.

4. Whisk in the eggs one at a time. Add the vanilla extract.

5. Gradually add the flour and salt, mixing until smooth.

6. Pour the batter into the prepared pan.

7. Bake for 30 to 35 minutes or until a cake tester or skewer inserted into the centre of the cake comes out slightly moist. Do not over-bake.

8. Cool completely before cutting into 2 x 2-in (5 x 5-cm) squares.

9. Serve or store in an airtight container at room temperature for up to 2 days. Keep refrigerated for a longer shelf life.

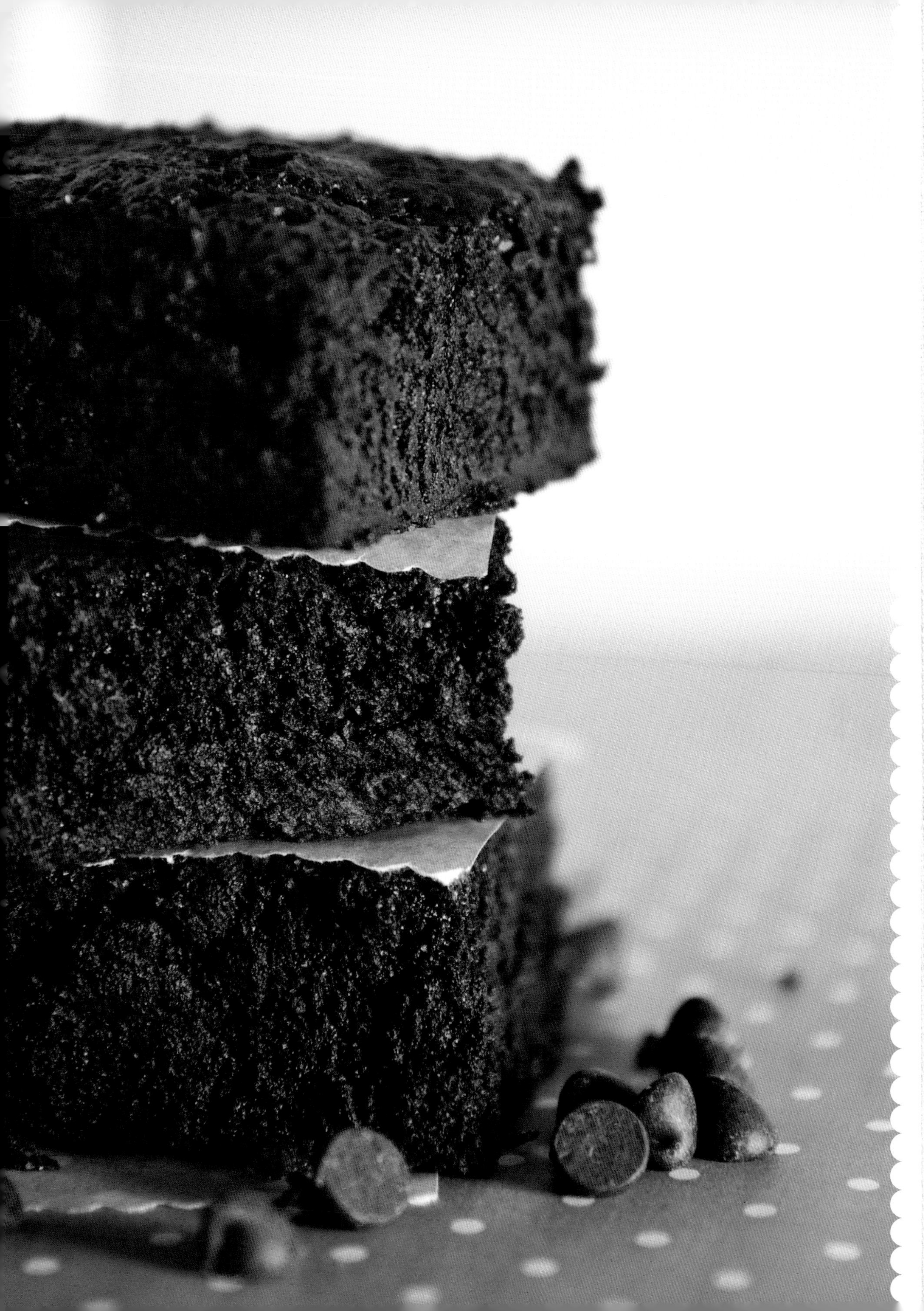

Food for the Gods

Also known as date and walnut bars in some parts of the world, this treat has many versions, but I guarantee that my recipe is worth indulging on.

Makes 30 bars

Ingredients

Butter	1 cup, cubed
Sugar	½ cup
Brown sugar	1½ cups
Eggs	3, large
Vanilla extract	1 tsp
Dates	1 cup, pitted and chopped
Walnuts	1 cup, chopped
Plain (all-purpose) flour	1¼ cups
Baking powder	½ tsp
Baking soda	½ tsp
Salt	¼ tsp

Method

1. Preheat the oven to 350°F (180°C). Grease and flour an 8 x 12-in (20 x 30-cm) baking pan.

2. In a medium saucepan, melt the butter over medium heat. Add the sugars and mix until combined.

3. Remove from the heat.

4. Add the eggs one at a time, beating well after each addition.

5. Mix in the vanilla extract.

6. Fold in the dates and walnuts.

7. In a separate bowl, whisk together the flour, baking powder, baking soda and salt. Gradually add to the butter mixture, mixing just until combined. Do not over-mix or the bars will be tough.

8. Pour the batter into the prepared pan. Bake for 35 to 40 minutes or until a cake tester or skewer inserted into the centre of cake comes out clean but not dry.

9. Cool completely before cutting into 1½ x 2-in (4 x 5-cm) bars.

10. Serve or store in an airtight container at room temperature for up to 2 days. Keep refrigerated for a longer shelf life.

Mango Walnut Bars

This recipe is similar to that of lemon squares (page 110), but dried mangoes make these simple yet delectable bars more flavourful and chewy while walnuts add an extra kick.

Makes 24 bars

Ingredients

Plain (all-purpose) flour	2 cups
Icing (confectioner's) sugar	½ cup
Butter	1 cup

Filling

Water	1 cup
Dried mangoes	7 oz (200 g)
Plain (all-purpose) flour	¼ cup
Baking soda	1 tsp
Salt	¼ tsp
Eggs	2
Sugar	¼ cup
Brown sugar	¾ cup
Vanilla extract	1 tsp
Walnuts	1¼ cups, chopped

Method

1. Preheat the oven to 350°F (180°C). Grease an 8 x 12-in (20 x 30-cm) baking pan.

2. Prepare the crust. In a food processor, combine the flour and icing sugar and pulse a few times. Add the butter, pulsing until a soft ball of dough forms.

3. Press the dough evenly into the prepared pan and bake for 15 to 20 minutes until golden brown.

4. Meanwhile, prepare the filling. Boil the water in a saucepan. Add the dried mangoes and cook for 10 minutes or until soft. Drain the mangoes and roughly chop in a food processor.

5. In a bowl, whisk together the flour, baking soda and salt.

6. In a separate bowl, combine the eggs and sugars.

7. Mix in the vanilla extract and mangoes.

8. Add the flour mixture, mixing until just combined.

9. Pour the mango mixture over the baked crust and spread evenly. Top with the walnuts.

10. Bake for 30 to 35 minutes or until the centre is set but not hard. Do not over-bake.

11. Cool completely, then cut into 2 x 2-in (5 x 5-cm) squares.

12. Serve or store in an airtight container at room temperature for up to 2 days. Keep refrigerated for a longer shelf life.

Strawberry Streusel Bars

Streusel literally means "something scattered" and that is exactly how these strawberry bars are made— by sprinkling the crumbly topping over the crisp pastry.

Makes 30 bars

Ingredients

Butter	1 cup, cubed
Icing (confectioner's) sugar	½ cup
Plain (all-purpose) flour	2 cups
Strawberry filling	1 can (21 oz / 595 g)

Streusel

Butter	⅓ cup, cubed
Sugar	½ cup
Plain (all-purpose) flour	1 cup

Method

1. Preheat the oven to 350°F (180°C). Grease and line an 8 x 12-in (20 x 30-cm) baking pan.

2. Prepare the crust. Combine the butter, icing sugar and flour in a food processor, pulsing until the mixture resembles coarse meal. Pulse a few more times until it just forms into a ball.

3. Press the dough into the prepared pan and bake for 15 to 20 minutes until golden. Remove from the oven and allow to cool for 5 minutes.

4. Spread the strawberry filling over the baked crust.

5. Prepare the streusel. Combine the butter, sugar and flour in a food processor, pulsing just until crumbly.

6. Sprinkle the streusel over the strawberry filling and bake for another 20 minutes.

7. Cool completely before cutting into 1½ x 2-in (4 x 5-cm) bars.

8. Serve or store in an airtight container at room temperature for up to 2 days. Keep refrigerated for a longer shelf life.

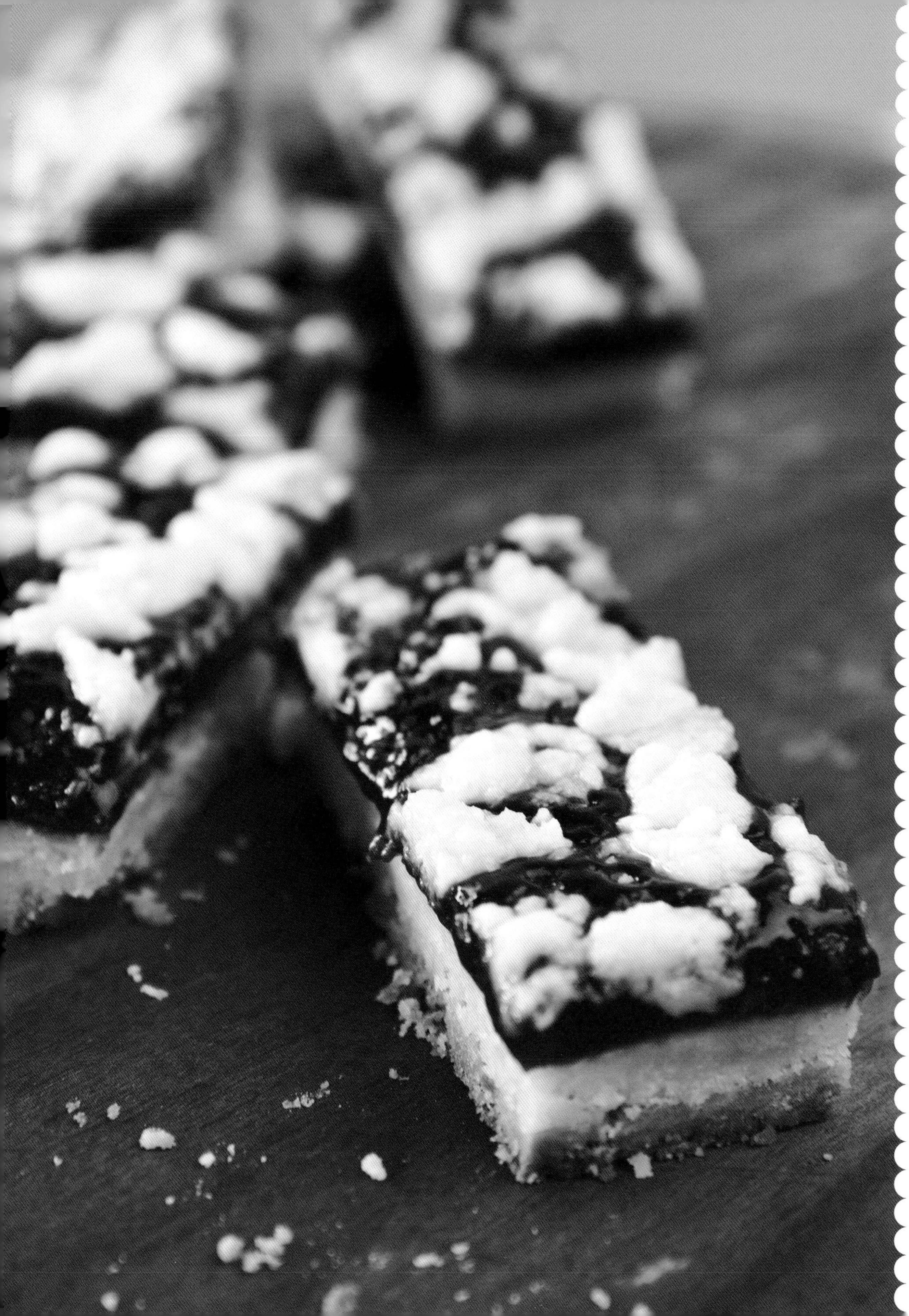

Rocky Road Brownies

Pure indulgence! These bars get their name from the unbeatable tandem of milk chocolate and marshmallows.

Makes 16 bars

Ingredients

Butter	1 cup
Unsweetened chocolate	1⅓ cups, chopped
Sugar	3 cups
Eggs	5
Vanilla extract	2 tsp
Plain (all-purpose) flour	1¾ cups
Salt	1 tsp
Mini marshmallows	2 cups
Walnuts	1 cup, chopped
Semi-sweet chocolate chips	½ cup

Method

1. Preheat the oven to 350°F (180°C). Grease and line an 8 x 12-in (20 x 30-cm) baking pan.

2. In a heatproof bowl set over a pot of simmering water, melt together the butter and chocolate. Remove from the heat and set aside.

3. Using an electric mixer, beat together the sugar, eggs and vanilla extract on medium speed. Reduce the speed to low and mix in the melted chocolate.

4. Slowly add in the flour and salt, mixing until just combined.

5. Pour the batter into the prepared pan.

6. Bake for about 30 minutes until the edges are dry but the centre is still soft.

7. Remove the brownie from the oven and top with marshmallows and walnuts. Bake for another 5 minutes until the marshmallows are puffed. Leave to cool completely in the pan.

8. In a heatproof bowl set over a pot of simmering water, melt the chocolate chips. Use a spoon to drizzle the melted chocolate over the brownie.

9. Refrigerate for 15 minutes or until the chocolate is set. Cut into 2 x 3-in (5 x 8-cm) bars.

10. Serve or store in an airtight container at room temperature for up to 2 days. Keep refrigerated for a longer shelf life.

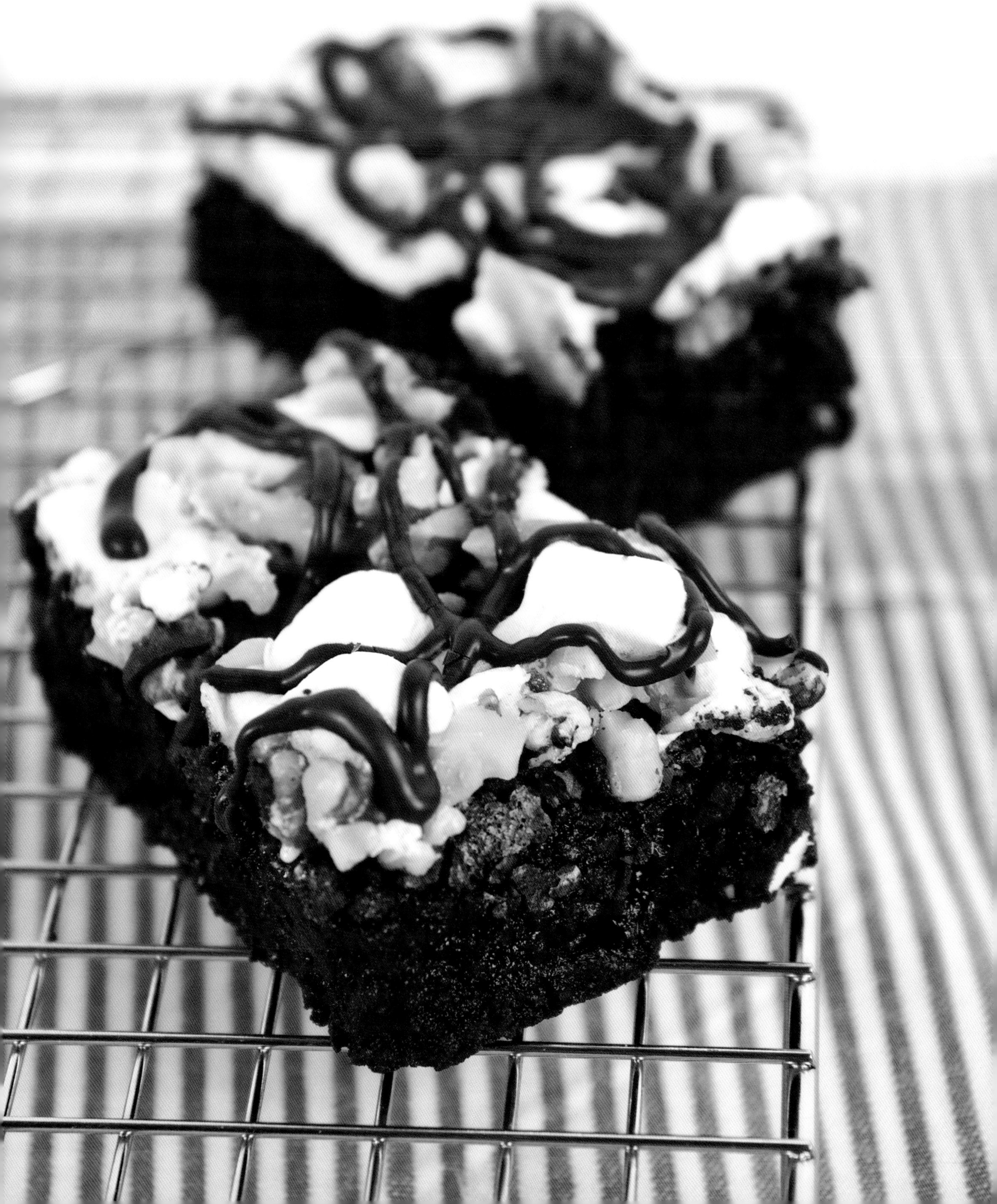

Raspberry Almond Meringue Bars

Enjoy a combination of textures and flavours in one bite—from the heavenly meringue, to the tart raspberry spread and the buttery almond crust. Lovely!

Makes 24 bars

Ingredients

Butter	1 cup
Sugar	1 cup
Eggs yolks	3
Vanilla extract	1 tsp
Plain (all-purpose) flour	2 cups
Baking soda	½ tsp
Salt	¼ tsp
Raspberry jam	1 cup
Flaked almonds	¼ cup

Meringue

Eggs whites	3
Sugar	⅓ cup

Method

1. Preheat the oven to 350°F (180°C). Grease and line an 8 x 12-in (20 x 30-cm) baking pan.

2. Using an electric mixer, beat together the butter and sugar on medium speed until fluffy.

3. Mix in the egg yolks and vanilla extract.

4. In a separate bowl, whisk together the flour, baking soda and salt. Gradually add to the butter mixture, mixing until a soft ball of dough is formed.

5. Press the dough evenly into the prepared pan. Spread the jam evenly over the dough.

6. Prepare the meringue. In a clean mixing bowl, whisk the egg whites on high speed until frothy. Gradually add the sugar, whisking until the mixture turns into a meringue with stiff and glossy peaks, about 5 minutes.

7. Spread the meringue evenly over the jam and top with flaked almonds.

8. Bake for 20 to 25 minutes or until the meringue is golden brown.

9. Cool completely before cutting into 2 x 2-in (5 x 5-cm) squares.

10. Serve or store in an airtight container at room temperature for up to 2 days. Keep refrigerated for a longer shelf life.

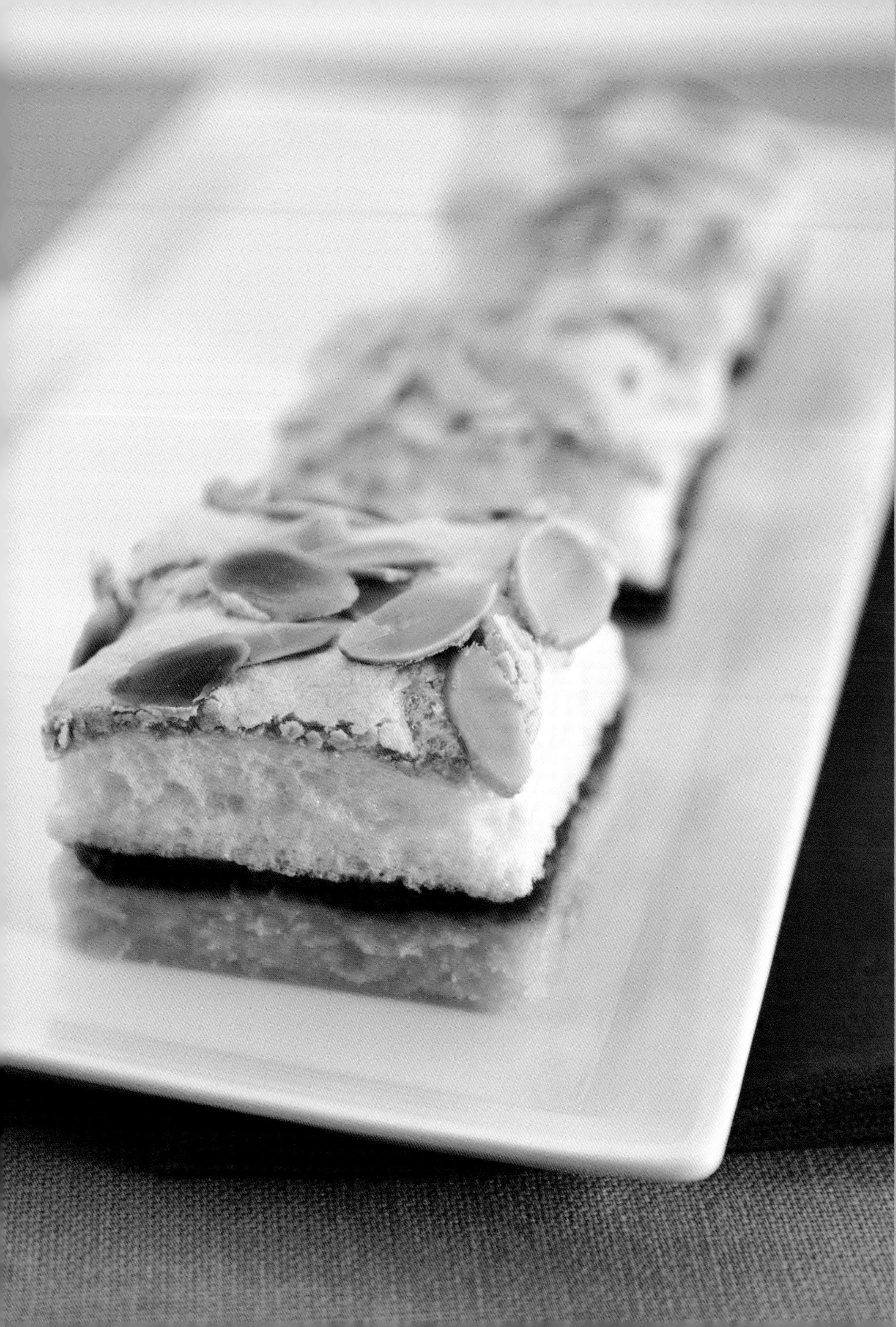

Chocolate Caramel Bars

There is something about the combination of gooey caramel and rich chocolate that makes these bars a hit. These are best enjoyed when the chocolate is firm and there is a slight resistance in each bite.

Makes 24 bars

Ingredients

Brownie Base

Butter	1 cup, cubed
Cocoa powder	½ cup
Sugar	2 cups
Eggs	2
Vanilla extract	1 tsp
Plain (all-purpose) flour	1½ cups

Caramel Filling

Butter	⅔ cup
Brown sugar	¼ cup
Corn syrup	2 Tbsp
Sweetened condensed milk	1⅓ cups

Chocolate Topping

Dark chocolate	1 cup, chopped
Vegetable oil	1 Tbsp

Method

1. Preheat the oven to 350°F (180°C). Grease and line an 8 x 12-in (20 x 30-cm) baking pan.

2. Prepare the brownie base. In a saucepan over low heat, combine the butter and cocoa powder, stirring until smooth. Remove from the heat.

3. Add the sugar.

4. Add the eggs one at a time, then the vanilla extract.

5. Mix in the flour until just combined.

6. Pour the batter into the prepared pan and bake for 18 to 20 minutes or until a cake tester or skewer inserted into the centre of the cake comes out moist but not wet. Remove from the oven and allow to cool.

7. Meanwhile, prepare the caramel filling. Heat the butter, brown sugar, corn syrup and condensed milk in a saucepan, stirring constantly until thickened and caramel in colour, about 30 minutes.

8. Immediately pour the caramel over the baked brownie base, spreading it evenly with a spatula or spoon, or by lightly tapping the pan against the work surface. Refrigerate for at least 1 hour or until caramel is firm.

9. Prepare the chocolate topping. In a heatproof bowl set over a pot of simmering water, combine the chocolate and oil, stirring until smooth.

10. Spread the chocolate topping over the set caramel layer. Refrigerate until the chocolate is set.

11. Cut into 2 x 2-in (5 x 5-cm) squares.

12. Serve or store in an airtight container in the refrigerator for up to 3 days.

Butterscotch Bars

Craving for something
chewy? Try this variation
of food for the Gods
(page 116). Use light or dark
brown sugar according
to your preference for the
colour of the bars.

Makes 30 bars

Ingredients

Butter	1 cup, cubed
Brown sugar	1¾ cups
Eggs	3
Vanilla extract	1 tsp
Plain (all-purpose) flour	1¼ cups
Baking soda	½ tsp
Salt	¼ tsp
Cashew nuts	1 cup, chopped

Method

1. Preheat the oven to 350°F (180°C). Grease and flour an 8 x 12-in (20 x 30-cm) baking pan.

2. In a medium saucepan, melt the butter over low heat.

3. Add the brown sugar and mix until combined. Remove from the heat.

4. Add the eggs, one at a time, beating well after each addition.

5. Mix in the vanilla extract.

6. In a separate bowl, whisk together the flour, baking soda and salt. Gradually add to the butter mixture until just combined. Do not over-mix or the bars will be tough.

7. Pour the batter into the prepared pan. Top with the cashew nuts.

8. Bake for 23 to 25 minutes or until a cake tester or skewer inserted into the centre of the cake comes out clean but not dry.

9. Allow to cool completely before cutting into 1½ x 2-in (4 x 5-cm) bars.

10. Serve or store in an airtight container at room temperature for up to 2 days. Keep refrigerated for a longer shelf life.

Quick Breads and Quick Bites

Chocolate Cupcakes

Chocolate overload! Chocolate in the cake, chocolate in the frosting and chocolate in the topping! Try saying no to that!

Makes 24 cupcakes

Ingredients

Cocoa powder	1 cup
Plain (all-purpose) flour	2 cups
Baking powder	2 tsp
Baking soda	1 ½ tsp
Salt	1 ½ tsp
Sugar	2 cups
Milk	1 cup
Vegetable oil	⅔ cup
Eggs	3, large
Vanilla extract	1 Tbsp
Boiling water	1 cup
Chocolate frosting (page 197)	1 quantity
Chocolate curls	as desired

Method

1. Preheat the oven to 350°F (180°C). Line two 12-hole muffin pans with paper cases.

2. In a bowl, whisk together the cocoa powder, flour, baking powder, baking soda, salt and sugar.

3. In another bowl, whisk together the milk, oil, eggs and vanilla extract.

4. Using an electric mixer, gradually add the liquid mixture to the dry mixture, beating on medium speed until combined.

5. Add the boiling water and beat for another minute.

6. Fill the lined pans with batter to about three-quarters full. Bake for 16 to 18 minutes or until a cake tester or skewer inserted into the centre of the cake comes out clean.

7. Meanwhile, prepare the chocolate frosting.

8. Transfer the cupcakes to a wire rack to cool completely before topping with frosting. Garnish with chocolate curls.

9. Serve or store in an airtight container in the refrigerator for up to 3 days.

Sticky Date Pudding

A sinful treat, especially when lathered with the thick and warm sauce. But it is so good, you will be stealing one bite after another.

Makes 12 small cakes

Ingredients

Dates	1¼ cups
Boiling water	1 cup
Butter	1 cup
Brown sugar	1 cup
Eggs	4, large
Vanilla extract	1 tsp
Plain (all-purpose) flour	1 cup
Baking powder	1 tsp
Baking soda	1 tsp
Ground cinnamon	1 tsp
Salt	½ tsp
Buttermilk (see Note)	¼ cup

Pudding Sauce

Butter	¾ cup
Brown sugar	1 cup
Liquid (whipping) cream	¾ cup

NOTE:
If buttermilk is not available, create a substitute by stirring 1 Tbsp vinegar into 1 cup milk. Let the mixture sit for about 5 minutes. The milk will thicken and curdle slightly. Use as a substitute for buttermilk.

Method

1. Preheat the oven to 350°F (180°C). Grease 12 small pudding moulds.

2. Steep the dates in a bowl of boiling water for 5 minutes. Drain and reserve ¼ cup of the liquid. Pulse the dates with the reserved liquid in a food processor until roughly chopped.

3. In a medium saucepan, melt the butter and brown sugar over medium heat.

4. Remove from the heat and add the eggs one at a time.

5. Mix in the vanilla extract and chopped dates.

6. In a separate bowl, whisk together the flour, baking powder, baking soda, ground cinnamon and salt. Gradually add to the batter. Add the buttermilk, mixing until combined.

7. Spoon the batter into the pudding moulds and bake for 12 to 15 minutes or until a cake tester or skewer inserted into the centre of the cake comes out clean.

8. Unmould the puddings.

9. Prepare the pudding sauce. In a saucepan over low heat, combine the butter, brown sugar and cream, stirring constantly until smooth and slightly thickened.

10. Spoon the sauce over the puddings before serving.

11. To store, leave the puddings to cool. Store in an airtight container at room temperature for up to 2 days.

Red Velvet Cupcakes

Make an impression with the robust colour and moist and velvety texture of these cupcakes. The addition of oil to the batter makes the cupcakes soft and yummy!

Makes 28 cupcakes

Ingredients

Vegetable oil	1⅔ cups
Sugar	1⅔ cups
Eggs	3, large
Vanilla extract	2 tsp
White vinegar	2 tsp
Red food colouring	2 Tbsp
Plain (all-purpose) flour	2⅔ cups
Baking powder	1½ Tbsp
Baking soda	1 tsp
Salt	1 tsp
Buttermilk (see Note on page 134)	1 cup
Cream cheese frosting (page 197)	1 quantity

Method

1. Preheat the oven to 350°F (180°C). Line three 12-hole muffin pans with 28 paper cases.

2. Using an electric mixer, combine the oil and sugar on medium speed.

3. Mix in the eggs one at a time.

4. Add the vanilla extract, vinegar and food colouring. Mix on low speed until the mixture is uniformly red.

5. In a separate bowl, sift together the flour, baking powder, baking soda and salt.

6. Add the dry ingredients to the batter alternately with buttermilk. Mix until well combined.

7. Fill the lined pans with batter until about three-quarters full.

8. Bake for 16 to 18 minutes or until a cake tester or skewer inserted into the centre of the cake comes out clean.

9. Transfer the cupcakes to a wire rack to cool completely before piping with frosting. Decorate as desired.

10. Serve or store in an airtight container in the refrigerator for up to 3 days.

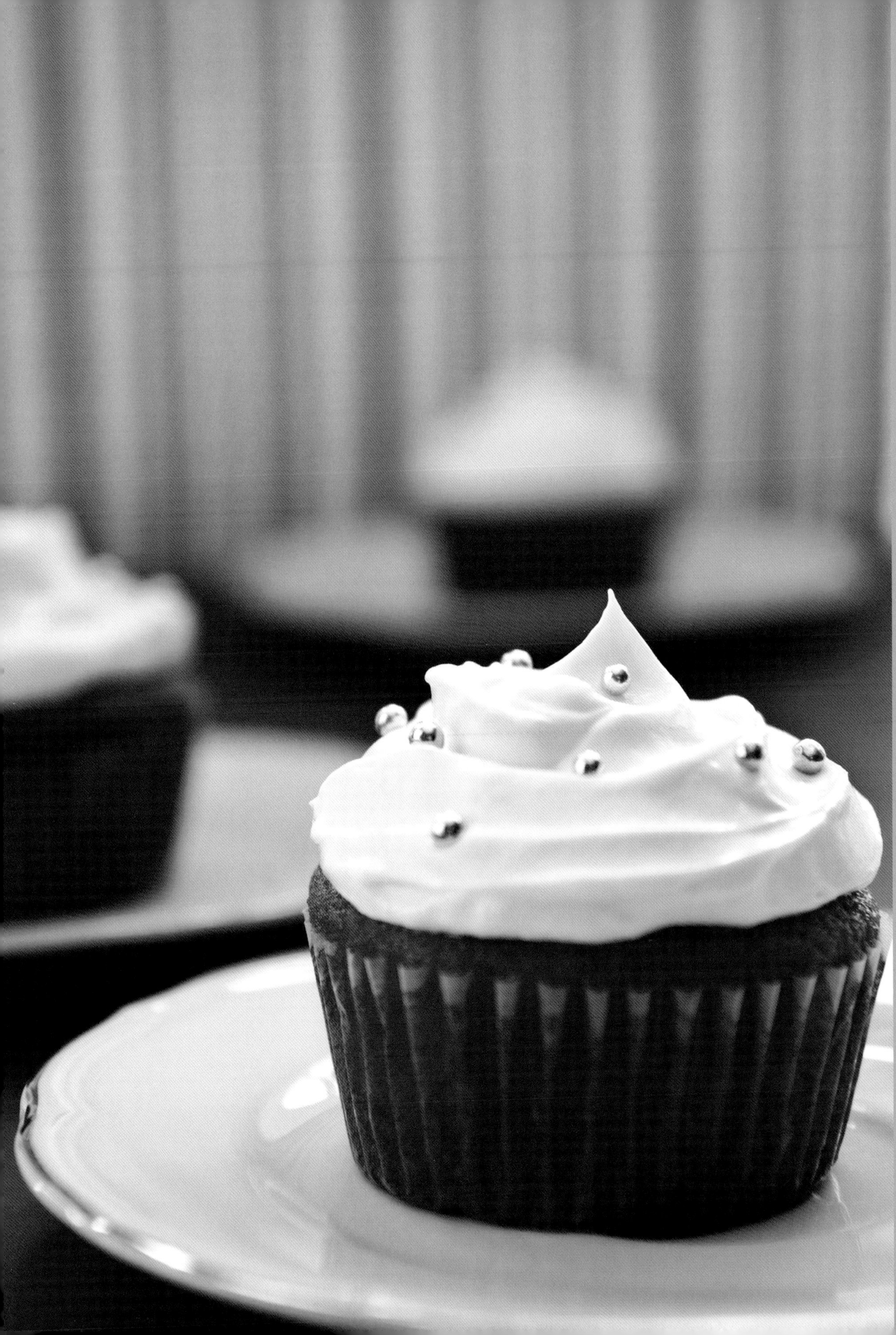

Lemon Poppy Seed Muffins

Poppy seeds provide a delicate crunch to this recipe. If unavailable, omit the poppy seeds for plain lemon muffins, or substitute with chopped walnuts or almonds.

Makes 12 muffins

Ingredients

Plain (all-purpose) flour	2⅓ cups
Sugar	⅔ cup
Baking powder	1½ Tbsp
Poppy seeds	1 Tbsp
Salt	1 tsp
Vegetable oil	1 cup
Buttermilk (see Note on page 134)	1¼ cups
Egg	1, large
Lemon extract	½ tsp
Lemon rind	1 Tbsp, chopped

Method

1. Preheat the oven to 375°F (190°C). Line a 12-hole muffin pan with paper muffin cups.

2. In a medium bowl, combine the flour, sugar, baking powder, poppy seeds and salt.

3. In another bowl, whisk together the oil, buttermilk, egg, lemon extract and lemon rind. Pour over the flour mixture and mix until combined.

4. Using a large (¼ cup / 2 oz) ice cream scoop, fill the lined pans with batter.

5. Bake for 20 to 22 minutes or until the muffin tops are golden.

6. Allow to cool for 15 minutes before serving.

7. Store in an airtight container at room temperature for up to 2 days.

Banana Bread

Pair this with your choice of coffee for a treat that is perfect morning, noon or night. Use very ripe bananas for a moist and scrumptious bread.

Makes one 9 x 5-in
(22.5 x 12.5-cm) loaf

Ingredients

Vegetable oil	¾ cup
Dark brown sugar	¾ cup
Eggs	2, large
Vanilla extract	1 tsp
Very ripe bananas	1½ cups, peeled and mashed
Plain (all-purpose) flour	1¾ cups
Baking powder	1½ tsp
Baking soda	½ tsp
Salt	½ tsp
Milk	½ cup

Method

1. Preheat the oven to 350°F (180°C). Grease and line a 9 x 5-in (22.5 x 12.5-cm) loaf pan with parchment paper.

2. Using an electric mixer, combine the oil and sugar on medium speed.

3. Add the eggs one at a time. Add the vanilla extract and mashed bananas and reduce the speed to low.

4. In a separate bowl, whisk together the flour, baking powder, baking soda and salt. Add to the egg mixture alternately with milk. Mix until well combined.

5. Pour the batter into the prepared pan. Bake for 55 to 60 minutes or until a cake tester or skewer inserted into the centre of the cake comes out clean.

6. Transfer to a wire rack to cool completely before slicing to serve.

7. Store in an airtight container at room temperature for up to 2 days.

Blueberry Muffins

My take on a classic. Make it a staple in your own home, just like it is in mine.

Makes 12 muffins

Ingredients

Plain (all-purpose) flour	2½ cups
Sugar	⅔ cup
Baking powder	1½ Tbsp
Salt	1 tsp
Vegetable oil	1 cup
Buttermilk (see Note on page 134)	1¼ cups
Egg	1, large
Vanilla extract	1 tsp
Frozen blueberries	2 cups

Streusel

Plain (all-purpose) flour	1 cup
Butter	½ cup
Sugar	½ cup

Method

1. Preheat the oven to 375°F (190°C). Line a 12-hole muffin pan with paper cases.

2. In a medium bowl, combine the flour, sugar, baking powder and salt.

3. In another bowl, whisk together the oil, buttermilk, egg and vanilla extract. Mix with the flour mixture until combined.

4. Fold in the blueberries.

5. Using a large (¼ cup / 2 oz) ice cream scoop, fill the lined pans with batter.

6. Prepare the streusel. Combine the butter, sugar and flour in a food processor, pulsing just until crumbly.

7. Top each muffin with about 1 Tbsp streusel.

8. Bake for 20 to 22 minutes or until the muffin tops are golden.

9. Allow to cool for 15 minutes before serving.

10. Store in an airtight container at room temperature for up to 2 days.

Vanilla Cupcakes

Time to be creative! Add any topping or frosting of choice to this classic cupcake. Here, I used Swiss meringue topping and red candy sprinkles.

Makes 24 cupcakes

Ingredients

Butter	1 cup, softened
Sugar	1⅔ cups
Eggs	4, large
Vanilla extract	1 Tbsp
Plain (all-purpose) flour	3 cups
Baking powder	2 tsp
Milk	1 cup
Swiss meringue (page 197)	1 quantity

Method

1. Preheat the oven to 350°F (180°C). Line two 12-hole muffin pans with paper cases.

2. Using an electric mixer, cream the butter and sugar until light and fluffy.

3. Add the eggs one at a time, beating each egg for about 1 minute.

4. Add the vanilla extract and continue beating until combined. Reduce speed to low.

5. In a separate bowl, sift together the flour and baking powder. Add a third of the flour to the batter, then half of the milk and beat until combined. Repeat this process. Add the remaining flour and beat until combined.

6. Fill the lined pans with batter until about three-quarters full.

7. Bake for 16 to 18 minutes or until a cake tester or skewer inserted into the centre of the cake comes out clean.

8. Transfer the cupcakes to a wire rack to cool completely before frosting with Swiss meringue. Decorate as desired.

9. Serve or store in an airtight container in the refrigerator for up to 3 days.

Apple Walnut Loaf

The contrasting textures of the apples and walnuts make for an interesting play in the mouth. Use a variety of apples that will not turn mushy upon baking.

Makes one 9 x 5-in (22.5 x 12.5-cm) loaf

Ingredients

Vegetable oil	1 cup
Sugar	1¼ cups
Eggs	2, large
Vanilla extract	1 tsp
Plain (all-purpose) flour	2 cups
Baking powder	1 tsp
Baking soda	½ tsp
Salt	½ tsp
Ground cinnamon	2 tsp
Milk	½ cup
Red apples	2, pared, cored and cut into ¼-in (0.5-cm) cubes
Walnuts	½ cup, chopped

Method

1. Preheat the oven to 350°F (180°C). Grease and flour a 9 x 5-in (22.5 x 12.5-cm) loaf pan.

2. Using an electric mixer, combine the oil and sugar on medium speed.

3. Add the eggs one at a time. Add the vanilla extract and reduce the speed to low.

4. In a separate bowl, whisk together the flour, baking powder, baking soda, salt and ground cinnamon. Add to the egg mixture alternately with milk. Mix until well combined.

5. Fold in the apples and walnuts.

6. Pour the batter into the prepared loaf pan. Bake for 55 to 60 minutes or until a cake tester or skewer inserted into the centre of the cake comes out clean.

7. Transfer to a wire rack to cool completely before slicing to serve.

8. Store in an airtight container at room temperature for up to 2 days.

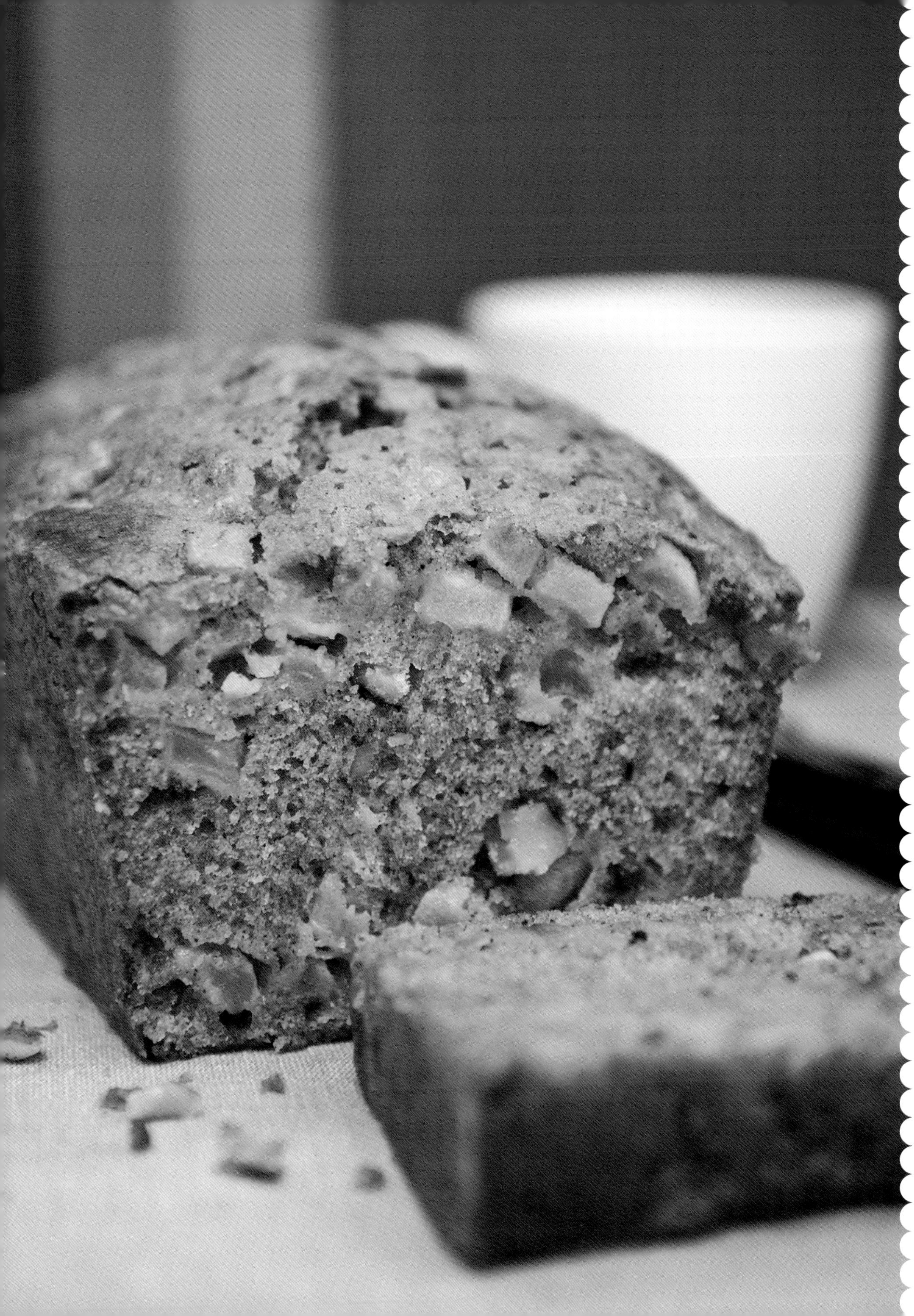

Marble Pound Cake

Bake a whole loaf! This pound cake makes a tasty quick bite for anyone on the go or when hunger strikes in the middle of the night!

Makes one 9 x 5-in
(22.5 x 12.5-cm) loaf

Ingredients

Butter	⅔ cup, cubed, at room temperature
Sugar	1 cup
Eggs	3, large
Vanilla extract	1 tsp
Plain (all-purpose) flour	1¾ cups
Baking powder	1 Tbsp
Salt	1 tsp
Buttermilk (see Note on page 134)	⅔ cup
Cocoa powder	⅓ cup
Boiling water	⅓ cup

Method

1. Preheat the oven to 350°F (180°C). Grease a 9 x 5-in (22.5 x 12.5-cm) loaf pan.

2. Using an electric mixer fitted with a paddle attachment, beat together the butter and sugar until light and fluffy.

3. Mix in the eggs one at a time, scraping the sides of the bowl after each addition. Add the vanilla extract.

4. In another bowl, sift together the flour, baking powder and salt.

5. Add the flour mixture to the egg mixture in three batches, alternating with buttermilk. Begin and end with flour mixture. Set aside a third of the batter.

6. Dissolve the cocoa powder in the boiling water and stir until smooth. Stir the cocoa mixture into the reserved cake batter until combined.

7. Spoon the batter into the prepared pan in two layers, alternating the vanilla batter and chocolate batter to create the look of a checkerboard. For the marble-effect, run a knife through the batter with a swirling motion.

8. Bake for 40 to 45 minutes or until a cake tester or skewer inserted into the centre of the cake comes out clean. Rotate the pan halfway through baking.

9. Transfer to a wire rack to cool completely before slicing to serve.

10. Store in an airtight container at room temperature for up to 2 days.

Cinnamon Swirl Loaf

Cinnamon gives this loaf a
lovely aroma.

Makes one 9 x 5-in
(22.5 x 12.5-cm) loaf

Ingredients

Butter	¾ cup, cubed, at room temperature
Sugar	1 cup
Eggs	4, large
Vanilla extract	2 tsp
Sour cream	1⅓ cups
Plain (all-purpose) flour	2½ cups
Baking powder	2 tsp
Baking soda	1 tsp
Salt	½ tsp

Cinnamon Sugar

Brown sugar	⅓ cup
Ground cinnamon	2 Tbsp

Method

1. Preheat the oven to 350°F (180°C). Grease and flour a 9 x 5-in (22.5 x 12.5-cm) loaf pan.

2. Using an electric mixer, beat together the butter and sugar on medium speed until light and fluffy.

3. Add the eggs one at a time. Mix in the vanilla extract. Reduce the speed to low.

4. In a separate bowl, whisk together the flour, baking powder, baking soda and salt.

5. Gradually mix a third of the flour mixture into the butter mixture, alternating with sour cream. Repeat the process, beginning and ending with the flour mixture and mixing until just combined.

6. Prepare the cinnamon sugar. Combine the brown sugar and cinnamon.

7. Pour half of the batter into the prepared pan and sprinkle with half of the cinnamon sugar. Using a spatula, swirl the cinnamon sugar around. Repeat with the remaining batter and cinnamon sugar.

8. Bake for 45 to 50 minutes or until a cake tester or skewer inserted into the centre of the cake comes out clean.

9. Allow to cool completely on a wire rack before serving.

10. Store in an airtight container at room temperature for up to 2 days.

Pies

Mango Cream Tarts

Let these tarts prove that mangoes and cream make for a perfect and delicious combination. Nothing is as satisfying as this pair combined with a flaky crust.

Makes six 4-in (10-cm) tarts

Ingredients

Flaky pie crusts (page 199)	6 round crusts, each 4-in (10-cm) in diameter
Mango purée	½ cup
Icing (confectioner's) sugar	2 Tbsp
Liquid (whipping) cream	1½ cups
Apricot jam or pastry gel	as needed
Mangoes	1 to 2, peeled and sliced

Method

1. Prepare the flaky pie crusts.

2. In a bowl, mix the mango purée and icing sugar until the sugar is dissolved.

3. Using an electric mixer, whip the cream on high speed until soft peaks form. Gradually add the mango purée, mixing until just combined.

4. Spoon the whipped mixture into the prepared tart crusts and even out with a spoon or spatula.

5. In a small saucepan, warm the jam or pastry gel over low heat.

6. Decorate the tarts with sliced mangoes and brush with warmed jam or pastry gel.

7. Keep refrigerated until ready to serve.

8. Store in an airtight container in the refrigerator for up to 2 days.

Strawberry Tart with Mascarpone Filling

Smooth and silky mascarpone and fresh sliced strawberries make this delicate dessert a surefire winner.

Makes six 4-in (10-cm) tarts

Ingredients

Sweet tart crusts (page 199)	6 round crusts, each 4-in (10-cm) in diameter
Strawberry jam or pastry gel	¼ cup
Fresh strawberries	2 to 4 cups, hulled and sliced

Mascarpone Filling

Cold mascarpone	1 cup
Liquid (whipping) cream	1 cup
Icing (confectioner's) sugar	⅓ cup
Amaretto liqueur	2 Tbsp

Method

1. Prepare the sweet tart crusts.

2. Prepare the filling. Using an electric mixer, beat the mascarpone, cream, icing sugar and amaretto liqueur on medium speed until firm peaks form, about 2 minutes.

3. Spoon the filling equally into the prepared crusts and spread evenly with a spatula.

4. In a small saucepan, warm the jam or pastry gel over low heat.

5. Decorate the tarts with strawberries.

6. Using a pastry brush, gently brush strawberries with warmed jam or pastry gel.

7. Cover and refrigerate the tarts for up to 1 day. Serve chilled.

Crème Brulée Tarts

A classic French custard encased in a flaky pie crust. The caramelised sugar on top gives these tarts a most welcome crunch.

Makes six 4-in (10-cm) tarts

Ingredients

Flaky pie crusts (page 199)	6 round crusts, each 4-in (10-cm) in diameter
Vanilla bean	1 pod
Liquid (whipping) cream	1⅔ cups
Egg yolks	4
Sugar	⅓ cup + more for sprinkling
Salt	¼ tsp

Method

1. Prepare the flaky pie crusts.

2. Using a paring knife, split the vanilla bean down the middle lengthwise, then scrape the seeds into a saucepan. Add the cream.

3. Warm the cream over medium-low heat, stirring constantly until bubbles form around the edge of the pan. Do not boil.

4. Remove from the heat and set aside to steep.

5. In a large bowl, whisk together the egg yolks, ⅓ cup sugar and salt until smooth. Gradually add the vanilla cream, whisking until blended.

6. Return the mixture to the pan and heat just until thickened. Do not boil.

7. Allow the custard to cool slightly, then spoon it equally into the prepared crusts. Refrigerate overnight.

8. Just before serving, sprinkle some sugar over the custard and caramelise with a kitchen torch. (Use according to the manufacturer's instructions.) Serve immediately.

Lemon Meringue Pie

The downfall of many a lemon pie is the overwhelming tartness of the curd filling. This recipe is guaranteed not to disappoint.

Makes one 7-in (18-cm) pie

Ingredients

Flaky pie crust (page 199)	1 round crust, 7-in (18-cm) in diameter

Lemon Filling

Egg yolks	4
Water	1½ cups
Sugar	1⅓ cups
Corn flour	⅓ cup
Salt	½ tsp
Butter	2 Tbsp
Lemon juice	½ cup
Lemon rind	1 Tbsp, grated

Meringue

Sugar	1 cup
Water	½ cup
Egg whites	4

Method

1. Prepare the tart crust.

2. Prepare the lemon filling. Whisk the egg yolks in a medium mixing bowl. Set aside.

3. In a medium saucepan, whisk together the water, sugar, corn flour and salt. Turn the heat to medium and boil the mixture, stirring constantly, about 1 minute.

4. Remove from the heat and gradually add to the whisked egg yolks, whisking all the time.

5. Return the egg mixture to the saucepan and cook over low heat for another minute, stirring constantly. Remove from the heat and gently stir in the butter, lemon juice and rind until combined. Pour into the prepared tart crust.

6. Prepare the meringue quickly and use while the filling is still hot. In a saucepan, dissolve the sugar in the water over medium heat. Turn up the heat and boil until the temperature reaches 238°F (114°C) on a candy thermometer.

7. Using an electric mixer, whip the egg whites on high speed until stiff peaks form.

8. With the mixer still running, gradually pour the hot syrup down the side of the mixing bowl. Continue beating until the mixture is just warm.

9. Spoon 1 to 2 cups of meringue over the hot lemon filling with a spatula. Create decorative peaks by allowing the meringue to stick to the spatula and pulling it upwards, repeating the process all over the pie.

10. Brown the peaks with a blow torch or place the pie in a preheated oven at 425°F (220°C) for 3 to 5 minutes until the meringue begins to turn golden at the edges and tips.

11. Allow the pie to cool completely before serving.

12. Store in an airtight container in the refrigerator for up to 2 days.

Peach Galette

This tart is easy to make, looks beautifully rustic and tastes oh so divine! Canned peaches are just perfect for this. You may also replace peaches with other fruit.

Makes 6 small tarts

Ingredients

Cornmeal Crust

Plain (all-purpose) flour	1¼ cups
Cornmeal	2 Tbsp
Sugar	1 Tbsp
Salt	½ tsp
Butter	½ cup, cubed
Shortening	¼ cup, cubed
Iced water	¼ cup

Filling

Canned sliced peaches	1 can (1 lb 13 oz / 825 g)
Sugar	¼ cup + more for sprinkling
Corn flour	2 Tbsp
Peach purée	⅓ cup
Egg	1, beaten

Method

1. Prepare the cornmeal crust. Combine the flour, cornmeal, sugar and salt in a food processor. Pulse to mix.

2. Add the butter and shortening and process until the mixture resembles coarse meal.

3. With the food processor running, add the iced water through the feed tube in a slow, steady stream, over about 20 seconds, until the dough holds together.

4. Transfer the dough to a work surface. Roll out and flatten the dough into a disc. Cover with plastic wrap and refrigerate for at least 1 hour before using.

5. Roll the chilled dough out between two sheets of parchment paper to ¼-in (0.5-cm) thickness. Cut out six 6-in (15-cm) rounds. Place on a sheet pan and refrigerate for 1 hour.

6. Preheat the oven to 375°F (190°C).

7. Prepare the filling. In a large bowl, mix the peach slices, ¼ cup sugar and corn flour.

8. Spread 1 Tbsp of peach purée on each dough circle, leaving a 1-in (2.5-cm) margin around the sides.

9. Top with peach slices, leaving the 1-in (2.5-cm) margin empty. Fold the margin over to create an edge and press gently so the dough does not unfold when baking.

10. Brush the dough with egg. Sprinkle some sugar over the peach slices.

11. Bake for 20 to 25 minutes until golden brown.

12. Transfer the tarts to a wire rack to cool for at least 15 minutes. Serve warm or at room temperature.

13. Store in an airtight container at room temperature for up to 2 days.

Black Bottom Banana Cream Pie

Bananas are available all year round. Use the Cavendish variety for this pie, as they remain firm longer. Spare some time to make this pie and you will be rightfully rewarded.

Makes one 7-in (18-cm) pie

Ingredients

Flaky pie crust (page 199)	1 round crust, 7-in (18-cm) in diameter
Pastry cream (page 198)	1 cup
Bittersweet chocolate	1/3 cup, melted
Liquid (whipping) cream	1 cup
Icing (confectioner's) sugar	3 Tbsp
Bananas	2 to 3, peeled and sliced
Chocolate shavings or curls	as needed

Method

1. Prepare the flaky pie crust and pastry cream.

2. Using an offset spatula or the back of a spoon, spread the melted chocolate evenly over the tart crust. Let the chocolate set in the refrigerator for 10 minutes.

3. Meanwhile, using a wire whisk or an electric mixer with a whisk attachment, whip the liquid cream in a mixing bowl until thickened.

4. Add the icing sugar and continue to whip until it forms medium-firm peaks. Set aside.

5. Remove the pie crust from the refrigerator. Spread the pastry cream evenly over the chocolate.

6. Arrange the banana slices over the pastry cream.

7. Using an offset spatula, spread the whipped liquid cream over the banana slices.

8. Garnish with chocolate shavings or curls.

9. Refrigerate for at least 3 hours for the pastry cream to set. Serve chilled.

10. Store in an airtight container in the refrigerator for up to 2 days.

Fresh Fruit Tart

A tart bursting with flavour and colour. Make sure to use a variety of fruit for colour and flavour.

Makes one 13 x 4-in
(33 x 10-cm) tart

Ingredients

Sweet tart crust (page 199)	1 rectangular crust, 13 x 4-in (33 x 10-cm)
Pastry cream (page 198)	1 quantity
Liquid (whipping) cream	1 cup
Strawberries	2 to 4 cups, hulled and sliced
Blueberries	1 cup
Canned mandarin oranges	1 cup, drained
Apricot jam or pastry gel	¼ cup

Method

1. Prepare the sweet tart crust and pastry cream.

2. Using an electric mixer, whip the pastry cream on medium speed.

3. Gradually add the liquid cream, whipping until soft peaks form.

4. Spread the cream mixture over the tart crust and refrigerate for at least 1 hour.

5. In a small saucepan, warm the jam or pastry gel over low heat.

6. Decorate the tart with strawberries, blueberries and mandarin oranges. Brush with warmed jam or pastry gel before serving.

7. Store in an airtight container in the refrigerator for up to 2 days.

The Best Apple Pie

A classic American dessert that combines a flaky crust with a scrumptiously juicy filling. Best served warm with a scoop of vanilla ice cream.

Makes six 4-in (10-cm) pies or one 9-in (22.5-cm) pie

Ingredients

Flaky pie dough (page 199)	1 quantity

Apple Filling

Granny Smith apples	6, pared, cored and sliced
Apple juice	¼ cup
Lemon juice	1 Tbsp
Sugar	¾ cup
Corn flour	¼ cup
Salt	½ tsp
Ground cinnamon	1 Tbsp

Method

1. Prepare the flaky pie dough.

2. In a large bowl, mix together the apples, apple juice and lemon juice.

3. In a separate bowl, whisk together the sugar, corn flour, salt and cinnamon. Mix with the apples, coating them evenly. Set aside.

4. Preheat the oven to 400°F (200°C).

5. For small or individual pies, roll the chilled dough out between two sheets of parchment paper to ¼-in (0.5-cm) thickness. Cut out 12 rounds from dough, each 6-in (15-cm) in diameter. Press 6 rounds into pie pans with 4-in (10-cm) holes. Set the remaining rounds aside.

6. For a large pie, divide the dough into two equal parts and roll each piece into 13-in (33-cm) diameter rounds. Gently press one round into a 9-in (22.5-cm) pie plate.

7. Spoon the apple filling into the crust(s). Lay the remaining dough round(s) over the filling, crimping the edges to seal.

8. Use any leftover dough to decorate the top of the pie(s). Make a few slashes or a hole on the pie top for steam to escape while the pie cooks, and to test for doneness later.

9. Bake for 15 minutes, then reduce the heat to 350°F (180°C) and bake for another 35 minutes or until the apples are tender. Test by inserting a skewer into the slashes or hole in the pie.

10. Transfer the pie(s) to a wire rack to cool for about 20 minutes before serving. Serve warm or at room temperature.

11. The pie(s) can be stored at room temperature for up to 2 days. Warm in the toaster oven at 300°F (150°C) for 10 to 15 minutes before serving.

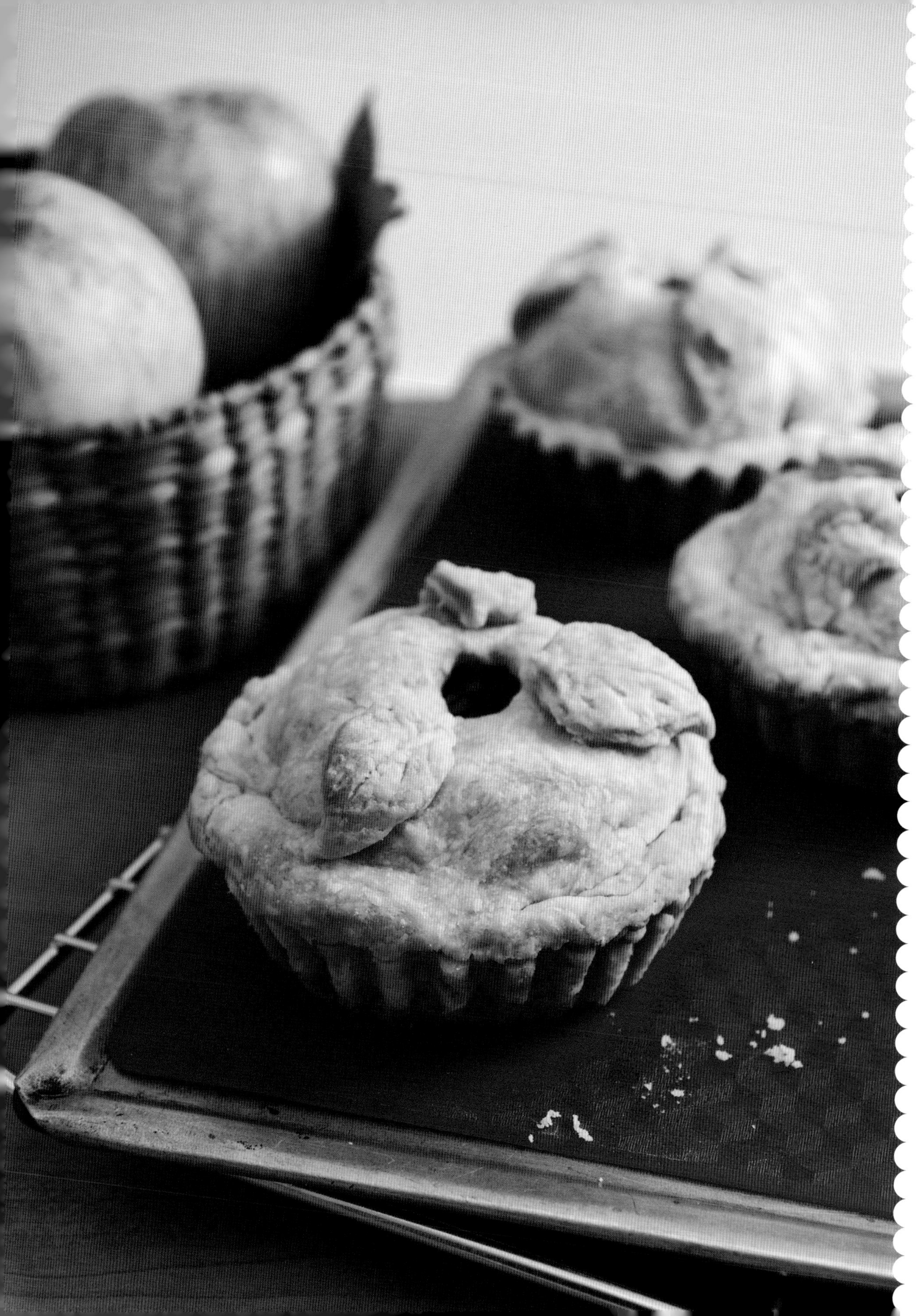

Pecan Pie

This classic pie is irresistible!
Be prepared for your friends
and family asking for more
helpings of this nutty pie.

Makes one 7-in (18-cm) pie

Ingredients

Flaky pie dough (page 199)	1 round crust, 7-in (18-cm) in diameter, unbaked
Butter	¼ Tbsp
Brown sugar	⅔ cup
Dark corn syrup	⅓ cup
Salt	¼ tsp
Vanilla extract	1 tsp
Cocoa powder	½ Tbsp
Egg	1
Pecans	1¼ cups ; ¼ cup chopped, 1 cup halved
Vanilla ice cream or whipped cream	as desired

Method

1. Prepare the flaky pie crust and leave unbaked.

2. Preheat the oven to 350°F (180°C).

3. In a saucepan, simmer together the butter, brown sugar, corn syrup, salt, vanilla extract and cocoa powder for 5 minutes. Remove from the heat and wait until slightly cooled.

4. Whisk in the egg and chopped pecans until blended.

5. Pour the mixture into the prepared crust and decorate with pecan halves.

6. Bake for 35 to 40 minutes or until the filling is set.

7. Allow the pie to cool for 15 minutes.

8. Serve warm with vanilla ice cream or whipped cream.

9. Store in an airtight container at room temperature for up to 2 days.

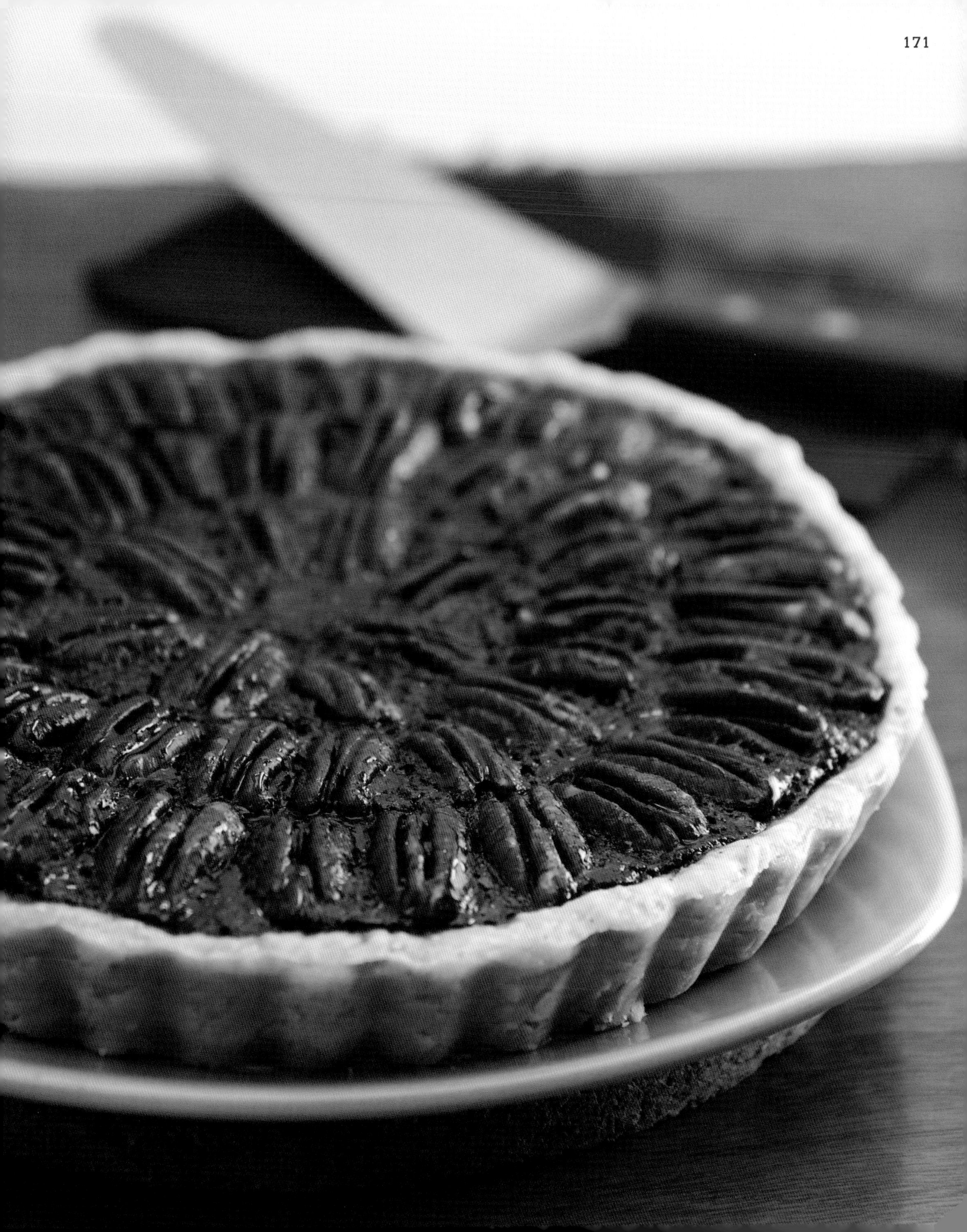

Turtle Pie

A dark chocolate cookie crust filled with chopped walnuts, drizzled with caramel sauce and topped with whipped ganache—a simply irresistible dessert!

Makes one 7-in (18-cm) pie

Ingredients

Crust

Dark chocolate sandwich cookies (such as Oreos)	1¼ cups, crushed
Butter	¼ cup, melted

Caramel Sauce

Sugar	1 cup
Water	2 Tbsp
Lemon juice	1 tsp
Liquid (whipping) cream	¼ cup

Ganache Filling

Semi-sweet chocolate	2⅓ cups, chopped
Liquid (whipping) cream	⅔ cup + 1 cup for whipping
Butter for glazing	2 Tbsp

Filling

Walnuts	⅓ cup, chopped

Method

Crust

1. Combine the crushed cookies and melted butter.

2. Press the mixture evenly into the bottom and sides of a 9-in (22.5-cm) pie plate. Refrigerate for at least 1 hour or until firm.

Caramel Sauce

3. In a heavy medium saucepan, combine the sugar, water and lemon juice and stir with a wooden spoon until the sugar is dissolved.

4. Cook on medium-high heat for 6 to 8 minutes until the mixture is amber in colour. To ensure even cooking, tilt the pan from time to time. Do not allow the sugar to burn.

5. Remove the pan from the heat and carefully add the cream, stirring with a long-handled wooden spoon until the sauce is smooth and blended. Take care that it does not splash as the syrup is very hot. Use heavy pot holders to protect your hands and arms.

6. Let the sauce cool to warm or room temperature. Refrigerate if necessary.

Ganache Filling

7. Place the chocolate in a heatproof bowl.

8. In a small saucepan, boil the ⅔ cup cream over medium-high heat. Pour immediately over the chocolate.

9. Using a whisk, stir until the chocolate is melted and smooth. Leave to cool until spreadable. Set aside ½ cup of the ganache for the topping. Refrigerate for at least 1 hour.

To Assemble

10. Place the walnuts into the prepared crust.

11. Drizzle with about ¼ cup of the caramel sauce.

12. In a mixing bowl, whip the chilled ganache until light and fluffy, then gradually add the remaining 1 cup cream and whip to soft peaks.

13. Spread the whipped ganache evenly over the walnuts. Freeze for at least 1 hour or until set.

14. Prepare the glaze. In a small saucepan, reheat the reserved ganache. Add the butter for glazing and stir until it melts and the chocolate is glossy. Pour over the frozen pie and tilt the pie so the ganache glaze is spread evenly.

15. Decorate with the remaining caramel sauce. Store in the freezer until ready to serve.

Cakes

Classic Cheesecake

This baked cheesecake makes a great foundation to a variety of cheesecakes, but is utterly delicious and just as sinful on its own.

Makes five 3-in (8-cm) cakes

Ingredients

Crust

Graham crackers	1 ¼ cups, crushed
Sugar	¼ cup
Butter	¼ cup, melted

Filling

Cream cheese	1 cup, softened
Sugar	⅓ cup
Eggs	2
Vanilla extract	1 tsp

Method

1. Preheat the oven to 250°F (120°C). Cover the base of five 3-in (8-cm) ring moulds with aluminium foil. Set aside.

2. In a bowl, combine the graham cracker crumbs, sugar and melted butter. Mix well.

3. Place about 2 Tbsp of the mixture into each ring mould and press down evenly. Set aside.

4. Using an electric mixer, beat the cream cheese on medium speed. Gradually mix in the sugar until well-blended.

5. Add the eggs one at a time, mixing well after each addition. Add the vanilla extract.

6. Spoon the filling into the ring moulds, filling each one three-quarters of the way.

7. Bake for 30 to 45 minutes until the filling is set. Turn the heat off and leave the cakes to cool completely inside the oven with the door ajar.

8. Serve or store in an airtight container in the refrigerator for up to 2 days.

Raspberry Swirl Cheesecake

This no-bake recipe is perfect for those who want to skip using the oven. The raspberry swirls make it both tasty and pretty.

Makes one 8-in (22.5-cm) cake

Ingredients

Crust

Graham crackers	1¼ cups, crushed
Sugar	¼ cup
Butter	¼ cup, melted

Raspberry Sauce

Frozen raspberries	1 cup
Sugar	¼ cup
Water	¼ cup

Filling

Cream cheese	2 cups, softened
Sugar	½ cup
Vanilla extract	1 tsp
Gelatine powder	2 tsp
Warm water	3 Tbsp
Liquid (whipping) cream	1 cup

Method

1. Line the sides of an 8-in (20-cm) ring mould with an acetate strip or aluminium foil and place over a sheet pan. Set aside.

2. Prepare the crust. In a medium bowl, combine the graham crackers, sugar and melted butter. Mix well.

3. Press the mixture evenly into the prepared mould using the back of a spoon. Set aside.

4. Prepare the raspberry sauce. Combine the raspberries, sugar and water in a blender and purée until smooth. Strain and set aside.

5. Prepare the filling. Using an electric mixer, beat the cream cheese on medium speed. Gradually add the sugar and vanilla extract.

6. In a separate bowl, stir the gelatine into the warm water. Leave for 2 to 3 minutes, then gradually mix into the cream cheese mixture.

7. In another mixing bowl, whip the cream to soft peaks.

8. Gently fold in half of the whipped cream into the cream cheese mixture, then continue to add the other half, mixing until combined.

9. Spoon half the mixture into the mould on top of the crust and level off with an offset spatula.

10. Spoon mounds of raspberry sauce onto the filling, starting from the edges and moving towards the middle, forming spots of raspberry all around.

11. Using a small spatula or knife, swirl the raspberry sauce around to form a design.

12. Top with the remaining filling and level off with a spatula.

13. Refrigerate for 3 to 4 hours to set.

14. Remove the cheesecake from the mould and peel off the acetate or aluminium foil before serving.

15. Store in an airtight container in the refrigerator for up to 2 days.

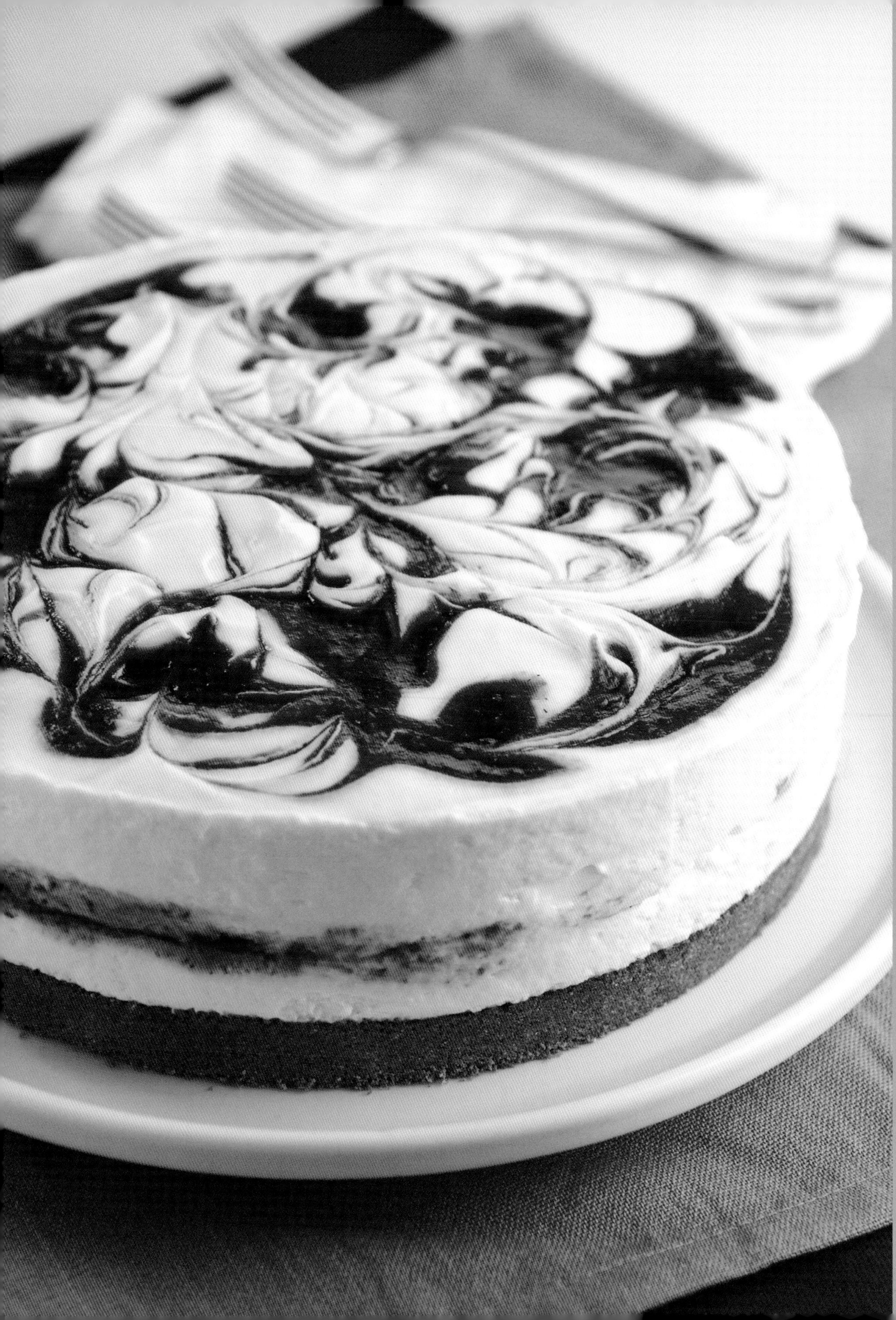

Pina Colada Cake

Fluffy vanilla chiffon sponges filled with crushed pineapple and coconut flavoured whipped cream! Try it!

Makes eighteen 3-in (8-cm) cakes

Ingredients

Vanilla chiffon (page 198)	1 quantity
Canned crushed pineapple	1 small can, drained
Toasted coconut flakes	as needed

Syrup

Water	½ cup
Sugar	¼ cup
Rum	¼ cup

Frosting

Liquid (whipping) cream	2 cups
Icing (confectioner's) sugar	⅓ cup
Coconut extract	2 Tbsp

Method

1. Prepare the chiffon cake.

2. Slice the chiffon cake into ½-in (1-cm) thick slices.

3. Using an 3-in (8-cm) ring mould, cut 36 rounds from the chiffon cake.

4. Prepare the syrup. Place the water, sugar and rum in a saucepan and simmer for 5 minutes. Set aside.

5. Prepare the frosting. Using an electric mixer, beat the cream to soft peaks. Gradually add the icing sugar and beat until stiff peaks form. Mix in the coconut extract.

6. To assemble, individually line 18 ring moulds, each 3-in (8-cm) in diameter, with acetate or aluminium foil.

7. Place a piece of chiffon cake at the bottom and brush with the syrup.

8. Top with 1 Tbsp frosting and 1 to 2 tsp crushed pineapple.

9. Repeat to layer with 1 Tbsp frosting and 1 to 2 tsp crushed pineapple, then top with another piece of chiffon cake.

10. Freeze the cakes for at least 2 hours to set.

11. Unmould the cakes and spread the top and sides of the cake with a thin layer of frosting. Coat with toasted coconut flakes.

12. Keep refrigerated until ready to serve. Store in an airtight container in the refrigerator for up to 2 days.

Honey Comb Crunch Cake

A light cake with an interesting mix of textures—crunch from the honey comb, a velvety feel from the whipped cream and a soft spongy bite from the chiffon. It is a surefire winner!

Makes one 9-in (22.5-cm) cake

Ingredients

Vanilla chiffon (page 198)	1 quantity

Honey Comb Candy

Sugar	1¼ cups
Water	⅓ cup
Honey	¼ cup
Light corn syrup	⅓ cup
Baking soda	1¼ tsp

Frosting

Liquid/whipping cream	3 cups
Icing (confectioner's) sugar	½ cup

Method

1. Prepare the chiffon cake.

2. Prepare the honey comb candy. Combine the sugar, water, honey and light corn syrup in a large saucepan. Boil until the sugar begins to caramelise or turns amber in colour.

3. Add the baking soda, using a wooden spoon to stir it in gently. The mixture will foam up.

4. Pour the mixture onto a nonstick mat or a piece of parchment paper on a sheet pan. Leave to cool completely before cutting it into pieces.

5. Prepare the frosting. Using an electric mixer, beat the cream to soft peaks. Gradually add the icing sugar, beating until stiff.

6. To assemble, slice the chiffon cake in half horizontally. Place the bottom half on a cake board or cake tray.

7. Spoon about 1 cup of frosting over the bottom half of the cake and spread evenly using an offset spatula. Add a layer of honey comb pieces, about 1 cup, then sandwich with the top half of the cake.

8. Spread the remaining frosting over the cake. Decorate the cake with the remaining honey comb pieces.

9. Slice to serve or store in an airtight container in the refrigerator for up to 2 days.

Carrot Cake

I learnt to make this while working in a pastry shop in California. Adding crushed pineapple and walnuts to the batter keeps the cake moist.

Makes one 9-in (22.5-cm) cake

Ingredients

Sugar	2 cups
Corn oil	¾ cup
Eggs	3, large
Vanilla extract	1 tsp
Carrots	1½ cups, grated
Canned crushed pineapple	½ cup, drained
Walnuts	1 cup, chopped
Plain (all-purpose) flour	2¼ cups
Ground cinnamon	1 tsp
Baking powder	1 tsp
Baking soda	½ tsp
Salt	½ tsp
Cream cheese frosting (page 197)	1½ to 2 cups

Method

1. Preheat the oven to 350°F (180°C).

2. Grease and line a 9-in (22.5-cm) round cake pan. Set aside.

3. Using an electric mixer, whisk together the sugar and oil.

4. Add the eggs one at a time, mixing well after each addition. Add the vanilla extract. Fold in the carrots, crushed pineapple and walnuts.

5. In a separate bowl, sift together the flour, cinnamon, baking powder, baking soda and salt. Gradually add to the carrot mixture, mixing until combined.

6. Transfer the batter into the prepared pan and bake for 45 to 50 minutes.

7. Remove from the oven and leave to cool completely.

8. Place the cooled cake on a cake board or cake stand. Spoon the cream cheese frosting over the top of the cake and spread using an offset spatula.

9. Slice to serve or store in an airtight container in the refrigerator for up to 2 days.

Orange Butter Cake

These mini cakes are buttery and moist with the aroma and flavour of candied oranges.

Makes six 3-in (8-cm) cakes

Ingredients

Butter	1 cup, cubed and softened
Sugar	1¼ cups
Eggs	4, large
Plain (all-purpose) flour	2 cups
Baking powder	1 Tbsp
Salt	½ tsp
Orange juice	¾ cup
Orange rind	2 Tbsp, grated

Candied Orange Slices

Sugar	1 cup
Water	½ cup
Orange	1, thinly sliced in rounds

Method

1. Preheat the oven to 350°F (180°C). Grease and flour six 3-in (8-cm) cake pans.

2. Using an electric mixer, cream the butter and sugar together until light and fluffy. Add the eggs one at a time.

3. In a separate bowl, sift together the flour, baking powder and salt.

4. On low speed, add the flour mixture to the butter mixture in three parts, alternating with orange juice and rind and mixing well after each addition.

5. Spoon the batter into the cake pans, filling them only three-quarters of the way. Tap the pans several times or use an offset spatula to level off the batter.

6. Bake for 20 to 25 minutes or until the cakes are golden brown and a cake tester or skewer inserted into the centre of the cakes comes out clean. Transfer the cake pans to a wire rack to cool completely.

7. Prepare the candied orange slices. Boil the sugar and water in a small saucepan. Stir until the sugar is dissolved. Add the orange slices and cook over low heat until the orange slices are translucent.

8. To serve, unmould the cakes and place them on individual serving plates. Top each cake with a candied orange slice and drizzle with some syrup.

9. Store in an airtight container in the refrigerator for up to 2 days.

Strawberry Shortcake

This is a light and fluffy chiffon sponge combined with whipped cream and sliced fresh strawberries— my all-time favourite!

Makes one 9-in (22.5-cm) cake

Ingredients

Vanilla chiffon (page 198)	1 quantity
Liquid (whipping) cream	3 cups
Icing (confectioner's) sugar	½ cup
Strawberries	2 cups or more, hulled and sliced

Method

1. Prepare the chiffon cake.

2. Slice the chiffon cake in half horizontally. Place the bottom half on a cake board or cake tray.

3. Using an electric mixer, beat the cream to soft peaks. Gradually add the icing sugar, beating until stiff.

4. Spoon about 1 cup of frosting over the bottom half of the cake and spread evenly using an offset spatula.

5. Top with a layer of sliced strawberries, about 1 cup, then sandwich with the top half of the cake.

6. Spread the remaining frosting over the cake and decorate with piped frosting if desired.

7. Top the cake with remaining sliced strawberries.

8. Serve or store in an airtight container in the refrigerator for up to 2 days.

Fallen Chocolate Cake

This looks like a cake gone wrong, but taste it and you will agree that this is no ordinary fallen cake!

Makes one 9-in (22.5-cm) cake

Ingredients

Bittersweet chocolate	2¾ cups, chopped
Butter	1 cup, cubed
Egg yolks	6
Vanilla extract	1 Tbsp
Salt	½ tsp
Plain (all-purpose) flour	⅓ cup
Egg whites	6
Sugar	1 cup
Vanilla ice cream or whipped cream	as desired

Method

1. Preheat the oven to 350°F (180°C). Grease and line a 9-in (22.5-cm) round cake pan. Set aside.

2. Melt together the chocolate and butter in a heatproof bowl set over a pot of simmering water. Stir until smooth. Set aside to cool to room temperature.

3. Stir the egg yolks into the cooled chocolate mixture one at a time. Add the vanilla extract, salt and flour. Mix well.

4. Using an electric mixer, beat the egg whites to soft peaks. Gradually add the sugar, beating until glossy and stiff.

5. Gradually fold the beaten egg whites into the chocolate mixture until combined.

6. Pour the batter into the prepared pan. Bake for 35 to 40 minutes or until a cake tester or skewer inserted into the centre of the cake comes out with a few crumbs.

7. Leave to cool completely before removing the cake from the pan.

8. Serve at room temperature with vanilla ice cream or whipped cream.

9. Store in an airtight container in the refrigerator for up to 2 days.

Rum Cake

This cake is usually served during the holidays in Europe. The rum gives this buttery, moist cake a kick and helps it keep for days.

Makes 12 small cakes or one 10-in (25-cm) cake

Ingredients

Plain (all-purpose) flour	2¾ cups
Baking powder	1 Tbsp
Baking soda	1 tsp
Salt	½ tsp
Butter	1½ cups, cubed, softened
Sugar	1¼ cups
Eggs	4, large
Vanilla extract	1 tsp
Sour cream	1 cup
Rum	¾ cup

Rum Syrup

Water	½ cup
Sugar	½ cup
Dark rum	½ cup

Method

1. Preheat the oven to 350°F (180°C). Grease and flour 12 individual 3-in (8-cm) cake pans or one 10-in (25-cm) bundt pan. Set aside.

2. In a mixing bowl, whisk together the flour, baking powder, baking soda and salt.

3. Using an electric mixer, cream the butter and sugar on medium speed until light and fluffy.

4. Add the eggs one at a time, beating well after each addition. Add the vanilla extract.

5. Reduce the speed to low and alternately add the flour mixture and sour cream.

6. Add the rum and continue mixing until blended.

7. Spoon the batter into the prepared pan(s).

8. Bake the individual cakes for 20 to 25 minutes and the bundt for 55 to 60 minutes. A cake tester or skewer inserted into the centre of the cake(s) should come out clean.

9. Leave the cake(s) in the pan(s) and place on a wire rack to cool for about 20 minutes.

10. Meanwhile, prepare the rum syrup. Combine the water and sugar in a small saucepan and simmer for 5 to 10 minutes. Remove from the heat. Stir in the rum.

11. Pierce the cake(s) all over using a skewer, then pour half the rum syrup evenly over the cake(s). Let stand for 30 minutes.

12. Unmould the cake(s) and leave to cool completely on a wire rack.

13. Brush the cake(s) with the remaining rum syrup before serving.

14. Store in an airtight container in the refrigerator for up to 2 days.

Super Moist Chocolate Cake

A slice is never enough! The icing might take time to make, but I guarantee it will be worth all the effort.

Makes one 9-in (22.5-cm) cake

Ingredients

Butter	1 cup, cubed, and softened
Sugar	1½ cups
Eggs	3, large
Vanilla extract	1 tsp
Plain (all-purpose) flour	2 cups
Cocoa powder	⅔ cup
Baking powder	1½ tsp
Baking soda	1½ tsp
Salt	1 tsp
Water	1⅓ cups

Icing

Cocoa powder	1 cup
Plain (all-purpose) flour	½ cup
Evaporated milk	2 cups
Sweetened condensed milk	1 cup
Butter	2 Tbsp

Method

1. Preheat the oven to 350°F (180°C). Grease, line and flour a 9-in (22.5-cm) diameter, 3-in (8-cm) high cake pan.

2. Using an electric mixer, cream the butter and sugar on medium-high speed until light and fluffy.

3. Reduce the speed to low and add the eggs one at a time, mixing well after each addition. Add the vanilla extract.

4. In a separate bowl, sift together the flour, cocoa powder, baking powder, baking soda and salt.

5. Alternately, add the flour mixture and water to the butter mixture, mixing until smooth.

6. Pour the batter to the prepared pan.

7. Bake for 45 to 50 minutes. Remove from the oven and leave to cool completely.

8. Prepare the icing. Combine the cocoa powder and flour in a medium saucepan. Gradually add the evaporated milk and whisk until smooth.

9. Add the condensed milk and cook over low heat, stirring constantly until thick.

10. Add the butter and mix until combined.

11. Unmould the cake and place it on a cake board or cake stand. Pour the icing over the cake and spread it out evenly using an offset spatula.

12. Slice to serve or store in an airtight container in the refrigerator for up to 2 days.

Basic Recipes

Sugar Syrup

Makes about 1 cup

Ingredients

Sugar	1 cup
Water	1 cup

Method

1. In a saucepan, stir the sugar and water over medium heat until the sugar is dissolved.

2. Allow to simmer over medium heat for 5 minutes.

3. Remove from the heat and allow to cool before using.

4. Sugar syrup can be stored in an airtight container in the refrigerator for up to 4 days.

Cream Cheese Frosting

Makes 3½ cups

Ingredients

Cream cheese	1 cup, softened
Butter	½ cup softened, cubed
Icing (confectioner's) sugar	2 cups, sifted
Vanilla extract	½ tsp

Method

1. Using an electric mixer, beat together the cream cheese and butter on high speed until fluffy.

2. Reduce the speed to low and gradually add the icing sugar ½ cup at a time. Add the vanilla extract and mix until smooth.

3. Use immediately, or refrigerate for up to 4 days. Before using, bring to room temperature, then beat on low speed until smooth. Use as required.

Chocolate Frosting

Makes 2½ cups

Ingredients

Butter	1 cup, cubed, at room temperature
Icing (confectioner's) sugar	⅓ cup
Salt	¼ tsp
Bittersweet chocolate	1¾ cups, melted and cooled
Cocoa powder	⅓ cup
Hot milk	¼ cup

Method

1. Using an electric mixer, beat the butter and icing sugar until light and fluffy.

2. Add the salt and reduce the speed to low. Gradually add the melted chocolate.

3. In a separate bowl, whisk the cocoa powder and milk until smooth.

4. Add to the chocolate mixture, whisking until blended.

5. If the frosting is too runny, refrigerate it for 5 to 10 minutes and whip again on low speed until smooth. Use immediately or keep refrigerated for up to 4 days.

Swiss Meringue

Makes 6 cups

Ingredients

Egg whites	4
Sugar	¾ cup
Salt	¼ tsp
Vanilla extract	1 tsp
Food colouring	a few drops

Method

1. Combine the egg whites, sugar, salt and vanilla extract in a heatproof bowl. Set over a pan of simmering water and whisk constantly until the mixture is warm to the touch and the sugar is dissolved.

2. Transfer the mixture to an electric mixer fitted with a whisk attachment and whisk on high speed until completely cool, and stiff and glossy peaks have formed. Takes 8 to 10 minutes.

3. Add food colouring to achieve your desired colour. Use as required.

Pastry Cream

Makes about 2½ cups

Ingredients

Milk	2¼ cups
Egg yolks	4, large
Sugar	⅔ cup
Corn flour	¼ cup
Vanilla extract	1 Tbsp
Butter	¼ cup

Method

1. Boil the milk in a saucepan.

2. In a bowl, whisk the egg yolks, sugar, corn flour and vanilla extract. Add half of the boiling milk to the bowl, whisking well.

3. Return the mixture to the saucepan, whisking continuously until thickened. Stir in the butter.

4. Remove the pan from the heat and transfer the cream to a bowl. Cover with plastic wrap and cool to room temperature. Refrigerate until ready to use.

Vanilla Chiffon

Makes one 9-in (22.5-cm) cake

Ingredients

Cake flour	¾ cup
Sugar	⅓ cup
Baking powder	1½ tsp
Salt	½ tsp
Corn oil	¼ cup
Egg yolks	4, large
Water	⅓ cup
Vanilla extract	1 tsp
Egg whites	4
Cream of tartar	¼ tsp
Sugar	⅓ cup

Method

1. Preheat the oven to 350°F (180°C). Line a 9-in (22.5-cm) round baking pan with parchment paper. Set aside.

2. In a medium bowl, sift together the cake flour, sugar, baking powder and salt.

3. In a separate bowl, whisk together the oil, egg yolks, water and vanilla extract. Add to the cake flour mixture, mixing until combined and smooth.

4. Using an electric mixer, beat the egg whites and cream of tartar on medium speed until frothy. Increase the speed to medium-high and gradually add the sugar, beating until glossy and stiff.

5. Gradually fold the whisked egg whites into the batter. Blend well.

6. Transfer the batter into the prepared pan and bake for 30 minutes or until the top of the cake springs back when touched. Do not prick the cake.

7. Remove the cake from the oven and allow to cool completely. Use as required.

Flaky Pie Dough/Crust

Ingredients

Plain (all-purpose) flour	2½ cups
Salt	1 tsp
Cold butter	¾ cup, cubed
Shortening	¼ cup, cubed
Iced water	¼ to ½ cup

Method

1. In a large bowl, mix together the flour and salt.

2. Add the butter and shortening. Using a fork or pastry blender, toss the flour to coat the butter and shortening, then cut in the butter and shortening until the mixture forms coarse crumbs the size of large peas.

3. Drizzle with a little iced water and continue tossing until the dough is evenly moist and comes together in a mass, but does not form into a ball.

4. Cover the dough tightly with plastic wrap and refrigerate for at least 1 hour or overnight before using. The dough may be stored in the freezer for up to 1 month.

5. Roll the chilled dough out between two sheets of parchment paper to ⅛-in (0.3-cm) thickness. Place the dough into the pie pan and press the dough into the edges. Gently prick the base using a fork. Repeat to line as many pie pans as required in the recipe.

6. Cover the pie pan(s) with plastic wrap and refrigerate for 20 to 30 minutes.

7. To bake, preheat the oven to 375°F (190°C). Line the dough with parchment paper, leaving a 1-in (2.5-cm) overhang all around. Fill with pie weights, dried beans or uncooked rice and bake for 15 minutes. Remove the paper and weights and bake for another 10 minutes or until golden.

8. Transfer to a wire rack and allow to cool completely. Use as directed in the recipe.

Sweet Tart Dough/Crust

Ingredients

Plain (all-purpose) flour	2⅔ cups
Sugar	¼ cup
Butter	1 cup, cubed
Egg yolks	2
Iced water	¼ cup

Method

1. Mix the flour and sugar in a food processor. Add the butter and pulse for 10 to 20 seconds until the mixture resembles coarse meal.

2. In a small bowl, lightly beat the egg yolks and add the iced water.

3. With the food processor running, pour in the egg mixture through the feed tube in a slow, steady stream. Pulse for no more than 30 seconds until the dough holds together without being wet or sticky.

4. To test the consistency, squeeze together a small amount of dough. If it is crumbly, add more iced water, about 1 Tbsp at a time.

5. Flatten the dough into a disc and cover with plastic wrap. Refrigerate for at least 1 hour or overnight before using. The dough may be stored in the freezer for up to 1 month.

6. To bake, preheat the oven to 375°F (190°C). Roll the chilled dough out between two sheets of parchment paper to ⅛-in (0.3-cm) thickness. Place the dough into the pie pan and press the dough into the edges. Place a large sheet of heavy duty aluminium foil over the dough, making sure to press the foil into the edges. Repeat to line as many pie pans as required in the recipe. Fill with pie weights, dried beans or uncooked rice.

7. Bake for 15 minutes until the crust dries out. Check if the crust is ready by pulling up one corner of the foil. If it sticks, return the crust to the oven and check every 2 minutes.

8. When the foil no longer sticks to the crust, carefully remove the weights by gathering the foil edges toward the centre and pulling it up and out. Reduce the heat to 350°F (180°C) and continue baking for another 10 minutes until the crust is golden brown.

9. Transfer to a wire rack and allow to cool completely. Use as directed in the recipe.